Nahid Tabatabaei

Being Forty

Translation: Amir Marashi

Editor: Liz Potter

AFTAB PUBLICATION
نشر آفتاب
2017

Aftab Publication
Hovinveien 37 F
0576 Oslo, Norway
aftab.publication@gmail.com
www.aftab.opersian.com

AFTAB
PUBLICATION
نشر آفتاب
2017

Nahid Tabatabaei

Being Forty

Translation: Amir Marashi

Editor: Liz Potter

aftab.publication@gmail.com
www.aftab.opersian.com

book identity

Name of book	Being Forty
Genre	Novel
Author	Nahid Tabatabaei
Translator	Amir Marashi
Editor	Liz Potter
Publisher	Aftab Publikation
Publishing year	2017
layout	Aftab Publikation
Cover design	Nadia Vyshnvka
ISBN	978-1981890576

All rights reserved translator

AFTAB PUBLICATION
نشر آفتاب
2016

For Firooz

She had become a pomegranate. A dried-up pomegranate left behind piles of rubbish in a storage room under the attic; if someone picked it up and shook it, they would hear the sound of its dried seeds. She could smell the staleness; a sweet, sour smell which would coagulate in the air; it would make the air heavy and would sit on her skin like a layer of sweat. She wanted to get up from where she was and run away. But she could only manage to move one of the fingers of her left hand; and with that movement she could feel one of the pomegranate seeds which was covered with juicy flesh. She tried again, and this time her right toes managed to pull in the cool edge of the sheet. She felt fulfilled. It seemed as if a sweet thought or memory had passed through her mind or her heart. Then she heard a sound. The sound was of a song. It was an old and familiar song which brought a sense of warmth and security with it. She could hear the song with her ears, taste it with her tongue, smell it with her nose and feel it with her hands. She could crush every single note between her teeth and taste their sweet and sour essence in the warmth of her mouth. It seemed as if someone had picked up the pomegranate from behind the pile of junk, opened the window and thrown it into the garden. Now all the seeds were covered with juicy flesh. She opened her eyes and closed them again against the glint of light. The music arrived and like a soft and tender shawl wrapped her around the shoulders. The shawl smelled of purple jasmine. She hummed the music and her life was revived. She could remember the music; the music whose player she used to love. She half-opened her eyes and stared through her eyelashes at the waves of light and shadow. Little by little the sound moved farther and farther away. Wakefulness was imposing itself on her. She was no longer a pomegranate. She was a young girl who had to get up and start a new day. She laughed. She was happy. She was happy because she was young, and happier for being in love.

She had to get up, wash her hands and face. She had to put on her socks and trousers. She would steal her father's navy blue and green check shirt and plait her hair. Two plaits, one on each side and a loop around her head; and then it was time for the conservatoire and classes and lessons, and the sound of music coming from behind the closed doors; like a paintbrush against the wall, she would move up and down the stairs, decorating the background.

She closed her eyes again and tried to remember the song; but it was not there any more. The song had got lost, and in its place she could see the black and white piano keys which – without any pressure from any fingers – were moving up and down without making a sound. Like a foetus inside the womb she drew herself in and once again remembered the dried pomegranate.

After a few seconds she became aware of the sound of the door handle turning, and looked towards the door. And there in the doorway, instead of her mother who woke her up every morning, was a man who was looking at her lovingly. The man smiled and said: "If you are awake, why don't you get up?" Suddenly the duvet felt heavy. It felt as if its weight had increased a thousand times and was pressing against her bones. She wanted to get up but couldn't. She closed her eyes again and saw that every scrap of memory was escaping from her mind. The piano keys, the plaited hair, the green and navy checks were hurtling away at an incredible speed and she could do nothing. She waited until the page in her mind became completely blank. She pushed the duvet to one side and sat up on the bed. This time the man opened the door and went to the wardrobe. He wanted to get dressed. She closed her eyes and whispered: "Farhad". It was as though she was introducing him to herself. Farhad turned towards her and said: "I've got three meetings today, I think we'll get a new contract, and if we do I'll buy you something nice". She thought: "Contracts, work, success, that's nice…" Farhad looked at her face attentively and said: "Don't you feel well?" She didn't answer. She got up and sat in front of the mirror and looked at herself. Farhad asked again: "Alaleh, are you all right?" She whispered: "I'm fine". But even to herself her voice sounded strange. In the mirror was a woman with short hair and a faint mark under her left eye, who was staring at her. All of a sudden the reality hit her hard. She was neither young nor in love. She was a woman of forty with dishevelled hair and a faded mark under her left eye. She put her hands on the dressing table, moved closer to the mirror, and stared into her eyes. She wanted to see herself in her own pupils. She wasn't there. She herself wasn't there. Farhad said: "Alaleh, do you want to stay at home?"

She touched her hair and said: "No, I'll go mad if I stay at home," and stood up.

Leaving the bedroom she saw Shaghayegh throwing the sofa cushions all over the place in search of her veil. As soon as she saw her mother she said: "Alaleh, will you lend me a veil?" Alaleh went back to her room and took a veil from the drawer. Once more she looked at herself in the mirror. She slid her glasses down her nose and said to herself: "The one who is young is your daughter," and left the room.

After they had dropped Shaghayegh off it began to rain. Heavy with the weight of the raindrops, the leaves had separated themselves from the trees and were falling slowly to the ground one by one. Alaleh bent her head and looked up through the windscreen. The branches of the trees on both sides of the road were touching, making a colourful dome over the pedestrians. She didn't feel like going to the office. She felt like walking on the wet leaves. She never felt like going to the office. She thought about the last time she and Farhad had gone out somewhere together. She couldn't remember. It had been a long time. She glanced at him furtively; he was cheerful and composed as usual. The sound of the cassette brought her back to the present. She was surprised at Farhad for the thousandth time. Nobody knew better than Farhad how she felt, and how to make her feel better. He always knew better than she did what she wanted to hear, what she wanted to say, and where she wanted to go. She thought: "Perhaps that is why he's so good at his job. He always recognises other people's needs before they do". The sound of the piano and flute filled the car, and Alaleh, remembering the pomegranate, turned towards Farhad. Looking at him affectionately she thought: "How different we are from each other, and yet how harmonious we are together". Farhad laughed and said: "I guessed right, didn't I?" And Alaleh knew he was now eager to see her reaction. She laid her hand on his knee and said: "It's been a long time since I heard it. Where did you find it?" Then she turned away and stared ahead. She couldn't say any more than what she had said. She knew that any other speech would be deceitful. Farhad opened the palm of his right hand and rested it on the seat. Alaleh gently placed her hand in his. Her hand was cold; she realised this because Farhad's was warm. Farhad lifted her hand towards his lips and Alaleh looked around anxiously. Nobody was paying any attention to them. People were hastily crossing the road and were only looking ahead.

She got out of the car at the top of the road to her office and stood there until Farhad was some distance away. Farhad waved to her. Alaleh put her hands deep inside the pockets of her *manteau* and watched the car as it moved off. Farhad sounded the horn and waved to her in the mirror. Alaleh smiled. She stood in front of a shop window and looked at the musical instruments displayed there. She still didn't feel like going to the office. She was thinking about getting a taxi to Tajrish and the Bazaar; she could wander among all the fruit and vegetable stalls looking at all those colours. Just then she felt the weight of a hand on her shoulder. She turned and saw Mrs. Shirazi, who was looking at her and smiling. She said hello and thought: "Now I will have to be a good employee: diligent, orderly, disciplined and cheerful". She tried to look normal and relaxed. Mrs. Shirazi held her arm and said: "We're five minutes late and you're standing here staring at that ugly *Tar* as lovingly as if you'd been playing the Tar for a hundred years. Come on, let's go, it's late." And she pulled her towards the office. As they moved away, Alaleh turned to look at the Tar in the window. Mrs. Shirazi pressed her arm and said: "Really, if I'm not mistaken you've fallen in love, in love with that big *Tar*," then she laughed loudly. Alaleh thought: "You have to have a mask for every person you know," and began to laugh at her own thought. As she swiped her ID card Mrs. Shirazi said: "Hurry up then, swipe your card".

Alaleh sat behind her desk and stared at the pile of files marked "Under consideration". The first file had a blue spotted cover. She knew very well that if she opened it, the first letter was about "Hormoz Shadan", and this was exactly the thing that was making her anxious and worried. When she had first seen the letter the previous day she hadn't believed what she was reading; but then she had read it three times and laughed at herself. Why should she have been surprised? Often in February leading Iranian artists who lived abroad would come home and perform in various concert halls. Why shouldn't he come? And then she had put the letter back in its file and stared at the calendar on her desk; she had stared and stared until her tears began to flow; her tea had gone cold and their boss had seen that she was doing nothing. And then, when a client had arrived, she had dropped the letter into the file and had attended to the client. But in a day or two she would have to read the letter and deal with it. She had to plan what was essential. She had to organise the rehearsal times and draw up the lists of names. She had two-and-a-half months, two-and-a-half months exactly. She pushed the file away and opened the day's newspaper. A bus had fallen into a canyon. A man had killed his wife. And they had announced the minimum wage for public employees.

In the evening, when they were all sitting around the dinner table, Farhad placed the dish in front of her and said: "Today you were not in a good mood". Alaleh looked at her fingernails and said: "I was tired; I didn't sleep well last night." And she thought: "I no longer play the cello, so why don't I grow my fingernails?" She put a little food on her plate and placed the dish in front of her daughter. At any other time Alaleh would have told Farhad everything; about the seeds of the pomegranate and waking up back in her youth. She knew he would listen to her attentively and understand everything perfectly. But now she was not in the mood. There was silence for a few seconds. Shaghayegh looked at her watch and said: "It's true what they say, that whenever there is silence the time is on the quarter hour; either a quarter to or a quarter past; and when it's on the half hour then it's two quarters…" Then she stopped, embarrassed for being a chatterbox.

The atmosphere in the room was oppressive. She thought it would be better to leave the two of them alone. Alaleh looked pale, and it was clear that Farhad, despite being cheerful as usual, was concerned about her. Shaghayegh thought: "As usual, he's totally focused on what has upset her," and suddenly she remembered an incident which had taken place that morning at university; and she really wanted to tell Farhad about it because she knew Alaleh was not in the mood. She turned her head towards her father and said: "Today in our sociology lecture Professor Sarmadi was talking about villages and showing some slides. Then suddenly we saw a flock of sheep and the professor was sitting on a rock among them; and one of the students from the back of the class said: "Sir, is that a group photo?" and the whole class burst out laughing. I was practically rolling on the floor laughing..." Alaleh knew that the story would now go on for ten or twelve minutes and she didn't need to listen, because Farhad was listening and asking all the appropriate questions, encouraging his daughter to continue in as much detail as possible. Slowly, slowly, Alaleh slid into the warm sheath of memory. "In those days he was tall and slim, when he played football he was the tallest and in the middle of the game I used to give him sweets, what children we were," and she smiled.

Shaghayegh, who was imitating Professor Sarmadi, thought Alaleh was smiling at her, so she prolonged her act. Alaleh looked at Shaghayegh, imagining her with plaited hair, and decided they were not at all alike. Why yes, her eyes were similar to her mother's, but her eyelashes and lips were like Farhad's; and the way she rested her chin on her hand and looked straight ahead was like Alaleh, but her hands were not at all like Alaleh's hands. Shaghayegh's hands were plump, with short square fingernails. If Hormoz saw her what would he say? Alaleh pushed her chair back and said to herself: "I wish at least she wouldn't cut her hair so short, and wouldn't wear all those silver rings in her ears. In our day girls were a lot simpler." She got up to take the dishes away. Shaghayegh, who was still busy talking, waved her hand and said: "I'll clear the table right away." But Alaleh didn't hear her. She picked up the large dish and moved towards the kitchen. Shaghayegh looked at her father in surprise and shrugged her shoulders. She finished what she was saying, then stood up and said: "I'm going to study." Farhad collected the glasses and went into the kitchen. He filled the kettle and said: "I'll do the dishes tomorrow morning. *Poirot*'s on tonight, you go and sit down while I make the tea." Giving in to his affection, Alaleh went and sat on the sofa. She knew he would wait until she decided to talk; and she also knew that, unless she wanted to, she didn't have to explain. And she knew that, sooner than expected, she would talk to him. In order to get rid of all these thoughts, she asked: "Well, what happened with the contracts?" He laughed and said: "I'll have to buy you something, it went very well. One of the managers in the company wanted to use his cousin, but Mr. Karbasi, who is the finance manager, sided with us..." Alaleh looked at him and tried to seem enthusiastic.

The following day, as Alaleh sat behind her desk, Mrs. Shirazi said the manager had come and told her that the arrangements for Mr. Shadan's visit should be made as quickly as possible. Alaleh placed the blue spotted file in front of her and stared at it, remembering a sentence she had written for Hormoz in the margin of a children's book "Shazdeh Koochoolo". It was where Shazdeh Koochoolo had told the man: "Am I not in one of the stars and am I not laughing in one of them? Then, when you look at the stars every night, it will seem as if all the stars are laughing. So you will have stars that can laugh." And she had written: "I do have a star that can laugh." She closed the file and murmured: "But the star was not supposed to come down from the sky..." From the other side of the room Mrs Shirazi said: "What did you say?" Alaleh laughed and said: "Nothing. I said stars were not supposed to come down from the sky." Mrs. Shirazi raised her eyebrows. Alaleh laughed. She knew Mrs. Shirazi was about to say: "You've gone crazy again."

Mrs. Shirazi slammed the drawer of her desk and said: "Hey, I'm going to report you, it seems you've gone crazy again. Yesterday you were staring at the shapeless frame of that Tar, and then today you're looking for stars." Alaleh shrugged and re-opened the file. She had to phone Hormoz Shadan's programme manager. She could phone Hormoz himself, but even the thought of doing so made her agitated. She put her hand behind her veil and pulled at her necklace. Then she picked up the phone, and as she dialled she thought: "I'm a weak creature"; and she remembered her fifth year teacher in high school, who was always upset by weak creatures.

She filled in a temporary absence form and put it on the secretary's desk. She said she had to go out, but would try to be back in a couple of hours. She had also told Mrs. Shirazi that she was going out for something, but despite her colleague's insistence had refused to say where she was going. Alaleh picked up her bag and left the office. As she reached the window of the music shop she stopped and looked at the *Tar*; she looked around her; there was nobody about. With her back to the street, and so close to the window she was almost touching it, she raised her hands. Then, pointing her index fingers at one other, she closed her eyes and moved her hands together. When she opened her eyes the tips of her fingers were touching. It was decided; she would go to Tajrish. She put her hands in her pockets and, for the last time, looked at her reflection in the shop window. She suddenly noticed the young man who was staring at her from behind the counter. She lowered her head and ran towards the top of the road, thinking: "Here's another person who thinks I'm crazy." To the first taxi driver who stopped she said: "Five hundred Toomans, Tajrish," then opened the back door and sat by the window. She realised that she was panting and her face was hot. She had spoken to the programme organiser, and when it came to introducing herself she had stammered. She didn't know what Hormoz would think when he heard her surname. Could the man pronounce it correctly? Was it at all possible that Hormoz would remember her surname? There were thousands of "Dashtis" in Tehran; how would Hormoz know that this one was her, after twenty years? She adjusted her veil, pulling it forward. She lowered the window half way and looked out.

The air was cool but not fresh; Alaleh thought about the air in Tajrish and breathed deeply. The Samsonite briefcase of the man who was sitting next to her was pressing against her knee; she huddled up a little and gazed out of the window. In the car next to them a young couple were teasing each other and laughing. Alaleh thought: "Why didn't I ever do things like that?" The young couple's car came to a stop next to the taxi; Alaleh became aware that the young girl had noticed her staring and realised she must have been looking at her disapprovingly. She thought: "I'm looking at her like an old spinster, but in my day we were completely different." And she remembered herself playing football in the yard with the boys, and smiled and turned her head and looked the other way. A small woman with a dark face stretched out her tattooed hand and asked for money. Alaleh looked at the motionless baby who was sleeping in the woman's arms and felt the cold sweat running down her back. She pulled the window up and involuntarily moved towards the other passenger. The corner of the briefcase pressed against her knee. The man gave her a surprised look and Alaleh thought: "Here's another one." The taxi started moving again. The young couple's car swerved very close to them and then pulled away. Once again Alaleh moved closer to the door and began to think: "I wish I could strangle all those women who lend out their babies," and she tightened her grip on her bag. The man glanced at her from time to time. Alaleh pulled her veil further down and said to herself: "It's not right to look at a woman like this. If they look at a forty-year-old woman like this it means either that her face is dirty or she's become ugly." The light turned red. On the pavement an old couple were walking together; they were both wearing black. Alaleh thought they must be going to a memorial service. The woman was wearing an old but clean black chador, while the man was wearing a suit which had been made many years ago. The hems of the trousers were very loose and the waist of the jacket was very tight. The man was wearing a colourless and faded trilby. The old couple suddenly decided to cross the narrow stream which ran along next to the pavement and step onto the road. The man took hold of the woman's bag; it was square and made of patent leather; it must have been at least forty years old. Alaleh laughed when she saw the man holding the bag. The light turned green and they passed the old couple; she felt they must love each other very much. She pulled at her necklace and thought: "Do they love each other, or are they just used to one another?" To love or to be used to someone: this is the problem; love or addiction? To love or to be in love? Who had said that to love is better than being in love? Whoever it was had said the most agreeable thing: he had said that being in love is often accompanied by excitement, thoughtlessness and sorrow; but loving is accompanied by steadiness, gentleness and logic. The man's briefcase was pressing harder and harder against her knee. She looked at the man and realised that the car had stopped and that the man was trying to get out, so she whispered an apology and got out. They had reached Pole Rumi. She got back into the taxi and stared at the trunks of the trees which, because of the empty road and the speed of the car, were flashing by very fast. On the other side of the seat, next to the window, was a young man who was sitting muttering to himself. Alaleh thought: "I hope I don't ever talk to myself like that," and touched her lips; they were not moving. Alaleh looked at the young man again and wondered: "Why is he talking to himself? Is he in love? Is he penniless? Is he unemployed? No, he's not in love, he's bored; he looks like someone who is bored; what would happen if I asked him what he's thinking about? I wish he would talk louder; he must be going to Tajrish as well." The car stopped. They had arrived. She paid the fare and got out. The young man got out too, and before Alaleh could follow him he was lost in the crowd. Alaleh decided to buy the first thing she saw that she liked. She opened her bag and counted her money. She could buy a pair of cheap shoes or a blouse. She closed her bag and was swallowed up by the black entrance of the Bazaar.

When she got back to the office it was midday. She felt lighter. She showed Mrs. Shirazi her blouse and waited for her to say she had paid too much for it, but instead she frowned and said: "You didn't say you were going shopping". Alaleh realised she had blundered. She said: "I had to go somewhere and do something, and then I bought this blouse. It was 2,000 Toomans". Mrs. Shirazi glanced at the blouse and said: "You paid too much". Alaleh laughed. Mrs. Shirazi always enjoyed telling her she was a novice when it came to shopping.

Later they had lunch together. After lunch Alaleh busied herself with filing her letters. She had to stay in the office until four thirty and she didn't want to think about anything. When it was time for the afternoon tea break, she and Mrs. Shirazi sat on one of the sofas in the middle of the room, drinking tea and eating dates. Taking the first sip, Alaleh noticed that

Mrs. Shirazi was looking at her searchingly. She realised that soon they would be having one of their two-hour chats. These chats would usually start with a few questions and then would go on and on until they reached a certain point which was the point Mrs. Shirazi wanted them to reach. Alaleh had no talent for this. As a matter of fact, she preferred to be the listener; she knew that Mrs. Shirazi needed to talk to someone and that she felt comfortable with Alaleh. Sharing a room for so many years had taught her that Alaleh could be a good and understanding friend. Mrs. Shirazi took a sip of her tea and began:

- You don't seem to have been feeling well the past two or three days.

Alaleh thought: "She always starts with me before she gets to herself," and replied:

- Well, you know I'm completely crazy.
- No, I'm serious. If I didn't know Farhad, I'd have thought he had upset you; or is it Shaghayegh who has some problem?
- No, poor things!
- Then what is it?

Alaleh, who was starting to get annoyed by the older woman's curiosity, suddenly made up her mind to tease her. Since they were going to have one of their little chats, she might as well have some fun. She put her cup on the table and stared at Mrs. Shirazi for a few seconds, then when she saw her waiting said:

- To be honest, I'm afraid of old age.

Mrs. Shirazi exploded:

- What? You're afraid of old age? You should be ashamed of yourself. If someone didn't know you, to hear you talking they'd think you were sixty.

Alaleh thought: "How loudly she talks; and the corner of her left eye is twitching, which means she's getting angry. She's saying sixty because she's getting on for fifty herself".

And she heard:

- What should I say then? You've only lived for forty years, what about me? If you look at what I've done in my life, I haven't even lived for ten. No travelling, no husband, no fun and no children... In the end they'll deposit me in the cemetery and nobody will even make halva and bring it to my grave.

Tears filled Mrs. Shirazi's eyes and Alaleh regretted starting this discussion. She got up, handed Mrs. Shirazi a paper hankie, and joked:

- Don't you worry, I'll cook halva every Thursday and bring it to your grave myself.

She tried to laugh, but Mrs. Shirazi hadn't heard her at all. Alaleh sat down and said:

- Come on, don't turn the waterworks. Instead of comforting me she's crying herself. Well then, dear, I made a mistake. I'm not old. I'm young - in fact I'm fourteen years old. Do you want me to put my head out of the window and scream: Hey people, I'm young!

Mrs. Shirazi wiped her eyes and said:
- Very well, stop fooling around. I only asked you what the matter was.

Alaleh, deciding to submit to Mrs. Shirazi's sympathy, pulled at her necklace and said:
- It's nothing, I'm just a bit confused.

Mrs. Shirazi, who was now feeling powerful, said:
- Nonsense, you have such a good husband, such a lovely daughter... Or perhaps you've fallen in love?

Alaleh got up from the sofa and went to the window. She saw the sparrows perched among the thin, bare branches of the trees; they had puffed up their feathers. The sparrows were exactly the colour of the branches. Alaleh thought: "Just like a ball of brown bouclé wool". Mrs. Shirazi asked:
- What?

Alaleh realised she had thought aloud and said:
- Nothing, husband and children are not everything in life; if they were you'd be dead by now.

And she fell silent.

As she spoke these last few words Alaleh's voice had cracked; Mrs. Shirazi realised that Alaleh too was choking with emotion, and that was why she was looking out of the window. She wished she could understand what the problem was. Alaleh had always seemed a little strange to her. Alaleh's sorrow made her both happy and sad. She felt happy because, despite all her good fortune, Alaleh still had problems; and she felt sad because she loved her. But curiosity was the most powerful feeling in her. She was in love with other people's problems, since her own had become stale to her. More than anything else she loved stories of love and disappointment, because she had been in love only once, and that had been many, many years ago. She still wanted to talk to Alaleh, but was aware that the other woman was not in the mood to talk.

The following day when Alaleh woke up she felt heavy and exhausted, as if she hadn't slept at all. Her mouth was dry and bitter. She looked at the clock. She would have to get up. She wanted to pretend to be asleep so Farhad would come and wake her up. She could hear the sound of the radio outside and the tap in the bathroom. She got up and sat in front of the mirror. She had a cold sore on the corner of her lip. She snorted and said: "This is just adding insult to injury". She pushed her hair behind her ears and then pulled it back over her face. Then she got hold of the tip of her nose and pushed it upwards, and pulled back the corners of her eyes, making herself look

Japanese. Then she put her hand under her chin and stared at herself. She sighed and said: "Thank God I was never beautiful, otherwise I'd be really miserable," and put some cream on her face. Farhad opened the door and said: "How are you?" Alaleh smiled and said: "Only average, and with a cold sore".

At the breakfast table Farhad and Shaghayegh were cheerful as usual. Farhad was teasing Shaghayegh, saying: "I hope to God you get married soon and go away. I am tired of making breakfast for you every morning," to which Shaghayegh replied mockingly: "Whatever you do, you do it for that woman with a cold sore and not for me," and they both laughed. Alaleh didn't laugh; she thought: "They're quite in harmony together, made of the same stuff; and they love each other more than they love me". Farhad and Shaghayegh, noticing her silence, didn't say anything more and busied themselves with breakfast.

In the car, when they were alone, Alaleh asked: "Have I aged a lot?"

Farhad gave her a look and said: "No, not at all, you are even more youthful than me". Alaleh turned and looked at him. He had lost some of his hair, which was also turning a little grey; he was chubbier than before, much chubbier. But he was still attractive. Alaleh said: "Sometimes I wonder what would have happened if I had married someone else and then met you somewhere?" Farhad lifted his head and looked at himself in the mirror; he pulled his moustache down towards his mouth and said: "Nothing, you wouldn't have paid the slightest attention to me". Alaleh was quiet and Farhad turned the cassette player on. The sound of the Tar filled the car. Alaleh turned the sound down and said: "You know, two or three days ago, just after I woke up, I was nineteen for a quarter of an hour". Farhad said: "I didn't like it when you were nineteen, because I wasn't there".

Alaleh took her ring from the third finger on her left hand, put it on the right hand and said: "No, you weren't, but I was in love; that is ... well that was it, I was in love. I was in love with a very tall boy with curly hair". Farhad hooted at a people carrier which had stopped in front of him. He put his head out of the widow and called out: "Hey, is this really the place to stop?" Then he looked at Alaleh and said: "When I was nineteen I was in love with football". Alaleh laughed and said: "Don't lie, boys fall in love every other day when they are young". Farhad opened his hand and laid it on the seat, but Alaleh ignored it. She got upset when Farhad evaded this kind of conversation. Farhad changed gear and said jokingly: "Do you feel really old then?" Alaleh said: "When you're young you think about old age in a different way. You think old age is a strange and odd condition which is a hundred kilometres and a hundred years away. But when you get there you see yourself as a fifteen year old whose hair has turned white; there are wrinkles around your eyes and your feet feel weak and you can't climb the stairs three steps at the time. And worse than anything else is the weight of the memories on your shoulders".

They had reached the top of the road where Alaleh's office was, but they still hadn't finished their conversation. Farhad drove on past the top of the road to make a detour. He felt that Alaleh still wanted to talk. Alaleh turned the mirror towards her and said: "Old age is just an ugly little mask that they stick on your face with a ton of adhesive. But behind it there's a young person who can hardly breathe. And then all of a sudden you realise you have become old and haven't done any of the things you wanted to do". Farhad thought: "She's thinking about university and her dreams and her music studies and…"

Alaleh tapped his knee and said: "What? What happened? What are you thinking about?" Farhad adopted a teasing tone as usual and said: "You're full of romantic talk today. Has something happened? I must come to your office and see what's going on. Or perhaps... Tell me, who's the lucky man? Tell me, and I promise I'll go to see him and declare your love for him". Alaleh put her bag on her knees and said: "Where's your manly pride?" Farhad turned towards her office and said: "Manly pride is for hardmen," and stopped the car. Alaleh opened the door; Farhad took hold of her arm and, imitating the manner of a thug, said: "I swear to you lady, we are nothing but the dust under your feet". Alaleh laughed a bit too heartily and got out of the car. Farhad said: "There's nothing going on, is there?" Alaleh laughed again and said: "Now you are just like Mrs. Shirazi, except that you don't have thin arched eyebrows." She looked at Farhad with a very serious expression on her face, and said: "Listen, you shouldn't get upset - when women turn forty they behave in odd ways. To prove that they're not yet old, they either get a boyfriend or wear strange clothes and dye their hair violet; or they go on a diet, or get pregnant again, or go to language school or...I don't know; but you can be sure that all of these only last for a very short period of time, and they soon get used to old age". Farhad said: "What about you?" Alaleh wound the window up and said: "I'll tell you one of these days." She was trying to shut the door when Farhad said: "Remember that you're not forty yet, there are still two or three months to go"

Mrs. Shirazi wasn't in yet. Alaleh pulled up the Venetian blind, put her bag on the table and left the room. Half way down the staircase she suddenly felt as if she was waking up; it was as if she had been sleepwalking. She put her hand on the stair rail and stopped. She was heading towards the auditorium without even being aware of it. Today a chorus was rehearsing in there; a number of religious anthems to celebrate the ten days which marked the return of Ayatollah Khomeini and the abolition of the monarchy in Iran in February 1979. She hadn't set foot in that auditorium for nearly fifteen years. In fact, since she had given up playing her instrument she couldn't bear watching other players. She would get particularly angry when she saw someone else playing the cello. Many times there had been concerts and Farhad and Shaghayegh had gone together; and when they had tried to insist she join them, she had answered: "That place is just my workplace, and no one goes to their workplace for pleasure". But today she was walking towards the auditorium and she didn't even know why. At the entrance the attendant saw her and ran towards her, saying : "Well, well, what a surprise to see you here!" Alaleh laughed and entered the main corridor, then very slowly ascended the stairs, opened the door to one of the balconies and sat down. Everywhere was dark and she knew very well that unless she made a noise no one would notice her presence. The auditorium was as beautiful as ever, with the same huge hive-shaped chandelier, red velvet seats and white railings. From high above, the women's veils and the men's black and white heads were continuously moving and making a noise. The players were like ants trying to carry pieces of food both small and large; bits of food that were refusing to be carried, and screamed, and wouldn't go. Alaleh moved forward a little and looked down. The cello was resting against a chair all by itself. She felt a tingling in the tips of her fingers. How many years was it since she had touched her instrument? She looked again. A few men and women came from behind the curtain and went to take their seats. There were still a few empty seats. Alaleh sat back on her chair and gazed at the ceiling. Hormoz used to say: "I hate sitting in concert halls where people make too much noise - they bend over and straighten up and cough, they drive me crazy". And now he was coming to perform in front of this very same audience.

She looked down once more and saw the reflection of light on the bald pink head of the flute player, and laughed. It seemed strange to her that someone should sit under the spotlights for other people to look at. Then she remembered sitting in front of a full-length mirror in her room playing the cello, and from time to time she would raise her head from her instrument and look at the position of her hands in the mirror. She never looked at her face. She rested her head on the cushion and remembered the last night before Hormoz's departure. There had been a party with many fellow students. The room was full of her and Hormoz's friends, and the girls were all over Hormoz, who was cheerful and witty and was teasing everybody. Alaleh sat in a corner, too sad to laugh at Hormoz's jokes. One day her mother had told her: "We've all been in love when we were young; loves which disappeared one after another, each one taking away part of our hearts". Alaleh thought about her mother's loves. How she would like to see some of them. And then suddenly she visualised a heart full of holes like a colander, and every piece had been taken away by someone. Alaleh smiled and thought she must remind her mother how much of her heart was left for her husband. She knew that the news of Hormoz's arrival would make her cheerful; just as any woman who knew of their old attachment would be pleased. And this was neither for Alaleh nor for Hormoz, but for all the young heartfelt loves which had gone and hidden behind the mountains and beyond the seas.

Now they were tuning their instruments. The musicians were making a lot of noise, moving their chairs to the right and left and turning the pages of their music. The women violinists were surveying each other as they bent over then sat up straight, while the double bass player was leaning against his instrument in such a way that it looked as though any second the instrument would slide away from him and he would hit the ground, chin first. Alaleh rested her elbow on the edge of the balcony; she was waiting for the cello player. She came in after everybody else; a fat woman with a round face. To Alaleh she looked like anything but a cellist; she looked more suited to lying on a sofa wearing a kimono. She looked like a fat spoiled cat, hardly taller than her instrument. At this moment someone called out: "Mrs. Saghafi" and the cellist turned her head. Her name was familiar to Alaleh and suddenly she remembered her. Sanaz Saghafi had been in the year below her; she was not very talented, but she was bumptious, very bumptious. Alaleh slid her glasses down to the tip of her nose and said to herself: "Why bumptious? I'm just jealous. She had perseverance and I didn't. Maybe if I'd continued I would be sitting in her chair now. I had no gumption and I gave up too easily. If I'd done what she did I'd be playing in Hormoz's orchestra now".

Tears slid down her cheeks and were buried in the creases of her veil. She got out of the chair and slowly left the balcony. And now she realised that this was the only thing she wanted. From the moment she had found out he was coming, without even being aware of it, she had wanted it from the depths of her being. Now, looking at the light outside the auditorium, this had become as clear to her as the daylight. She felt she had been humiliated and had been separated from the only thing she wanted. She left the auditorium and went quickly down the stairs, stamping her heels hard on the carpet; but she couldn't hear the sound she longed for.

Back in her room she went straight to her chair and picked up her address book. She took no notice of Mrs. Shirazi, who was staring at her with wide eyes. Alaleh turned the pages of the address book and looked under the letter M for the name of one of her fellow students. She found the number. She was very curious to find out more about Sanaz Saghafi. Her friend knew everybody. She dialled the number. After a few rings she heard the recorded voice of a child saying: "We are not at home, please leave your message after the tone". Alaleh paused for a little while then put the phone down. Immediately the phone rang. She picked it up and heard a voice at exactly the same moment as Mrs. Shirazi said: "Hi, lovely lady." Alaleh, who had only just noticed Mrs. Shirazi, glanced over at her and said: "Hello?" and then involuntarily "Goodbye" into the mouthpiece, and put the phone down. This made them both burst out laughing and Alaleh felt her mood lifting. When she stopped laughing Mrs. Shirazi said: "Now who was that you were calling?" For a moment Alaleh thought about telling her everything, but checked herself. She didn't want Mrs. Shirazi to know about her feelings towards Sanaz Saghafi. So she shook her head and said: "Nothing, it wasn't important". She opened her file and dealt with a few official letters.

By the time she arrived home in the late afternoon a thousand and one thoughts had passed through her head. Shaghayegh had a lecture and Farhad would not get home before eight o'clock. She had four hours to do what she pleased. She could catch up with some housework; she could lie down and watch television, or prepare a nice meal. She opened the door to the hall and breathed sigh of relief. She went into the bedroom, threw her bag and veil on the bed and lay on the bed in her manteau. She was tired. She closed her eyes and tried not to think about anything. She removed the pillow from under her head and stretched out her arms. Gradually she fell into a dreamlike state, a state in which thoughts are replaced by images. Fragmentary images which, one after another, become entangled with thoughts; and as soon as you try to follow them they escape from your memory and leave behind a sensation, either pleasant or unpleasant. At first, Alaleh saw herself in a long wide swimming pool, swimming with a gigantic fish. Then she saw Shaghayegh, who was combing her hair in the wind. She saw Farhad and Hormoz playing tag. And then everything got mixed up. She drifted off and once more heard the same song; the same old song that Hormoz had composed for her in the days when they preferred to communicate by exchanging sheets of music rather than by speaking. Alaleh gave herself up to the gentle murmur of the music and felt she was getting lighter and flying like a kite. Suddenly the music was interrupted and she saw the face of Mrs. Saghafi on another kite, laughing at her. The kite had two long streamers and Hormoz was holding its string. Alaleh felt she was crashing onto the bed and then a knock on the door brought her back to the present. She sat up. Her whole body was covered with sweat. She got up and went into the kitchen. Her heart was beating faster and she felt as if she would like to go up to the rooftop and inhale all of the air in the world. She drank a glass of cold water. She went to take a packet of meat out of the freezer but then forgot what she was doing. She shut the freezer door and went into the store room. Now she knew exactly what she wanted to do. She opened the store room door, moved a few suitcases and boxes out of the way and picked up the case containing her instrument. She went back into the bedroom and sat down in front of the mirror. She took the instrument out of its case and put her arms around it. She felt the upper part of the instrument smooth and straight under her hand and then, with a bow half of whose hairs were hanging off, she began to play one of the tunes she still remembered. After a few minutes she was so engrossed that nothing was important; neither the broken bow and nor the out of place bridge nor Mrs. Saghafi; not even Hormoz. There was only her and her instrument. She played one thing after another. It seemed as if all the tunes that she had forgotten for so many years had returned and were queuing behind a door, entering one by one and asking how she was. Alaleh was overwhelmed by the number of tunes she could still remember and her tears made a groove on the instrument's dusty body. As she played she glanced at herself in the mirror from time to time; her eyes were shining with happiness.

As she was playing one of her favourite tunes several times over she felt an extraordinary tranquillity taking over her very existence; she looked into the mirror and this time she saw herself in her own eyes. She smiled at herself then suddenly caught sight of something moving behind her reflection. She took the bow off the strings and looked behind her. Two heads, one black and one white, disappeared from the doorway. Anxiously she called out: "Farhad... Shaghayegh..." and stood up. As she got to the door Farhad hugged her and Shaghayegh started kissing her. Alaleh panicked and said: "I was cleaning the store room and I thought this instrument too..." Shaghayegh interrupted her: "So I thought, never mind the store room, let the suitcases and boxes stay in the middle of the hallway, and instead I'll sit down and hold my instrument, and never mind if my manteau is covered in dirt and my face is covered with dust and..." Alaleh sat on the bed and said: "I just wanted to see if it still makes a sound or not." She looked at Farhad and saw that he was telling her with his eyes: "Don't fool around". She stood up and said: "I'm going to take a shower." Looking in the bathroom mirror she saw the traces of her tears on her dusty face and realised that she had never been able to tell lies.

When she came out of the bathroom the tea was ready and Farhad was preparing one of his concoctions for dinner. It was one of those dishes that he would later give a Chinese name to. Alaleh looked at the clock on the wall and saw that it was half past eight and she hadn't even thought about cooking dinner. She got dressed and lay on the sofa. She was feeling calm and light. She wanted to sleep, so she lay and stared at the television.

From the kitchen Farhad said: "It will be ready in a minute, your highness. The name of this dish is Xiang Lang and it is cooked in upper Canton". Shaghayegh, who was setting the table, said: "Do they cook it and eat it or throw it away?" Farhad replied: "In the house where women do not cook, Xiang Lang should be praised". Shaghayegh laughed and said: "They don't eat it then?"

Eventually Farhad arrived carrying a large dish full of vegetables and pieces of chicken and, pulling a face, said: "And now here is Xiang Lang". Alaleh had to force herself to sit at the table, but as soon as she took the first mouthful she realised how hungry she was.

After dinner Alaleh knew she had to say something about what had happened. Farhad's face wore a mingled look of surprise, encouragement and sarcasm, while Shaghayegh was taking her time to clear the table so she could find out what happened. Alaleh had talked to Farhad about Hormoz in the past, but didn't know how he would react to the news that he was coming back. When they had talked about it all those years ago, no one expected Hormoz to become such a big star. In any case Farhad would know of his coming and then this secrecy would seem stupid.

Alaleh lay down on the sofa again and rested her head on her hands, wishing *Poirot* was on tonight so she could use that as an excuse to avoid the issue.

She was still thinking when Farhad took the initiative by closing off her escape route. He arranged the cushions behind him, lay back and said: "Very soon you will get something nice". Alaleh didn't reply. Farhad lit a cigarette and said: "In my opinion you change completely when you play". Alaleh laughed and said: "Younger?"

Farhad blew cigarette smoke through his nose and said: "Younger, more beautiful, stronger, and at the same time much more delicate". Shaghayegh, who was coming out of the kitchen biting into an apple, turned towards her room when she heard Farhad's heartfelt words, saying: "I have to study".

There, near the door, she could observe what was going on.

Alaleh stood up and then sat down again. She wound the belt of her dress around her finger and said: "Today I went to the auditorium for the first time for many years. There was a rehearsal going on. I went to the balcony and watched. I wanted to know who was playing the cello; then I saw a round, plump girl from the year below us come and tune the instrument. And then I remembered that that girl, that woman, had never shown any talent, but now…" Farhad fidgeted in his chair and said: "But now?" Alaleh unwound the belt from her finger and said: "Well, I could easily have been in her place…" Farhad put out his cigarette and said: "And then?" Alaleh let go of the belt, stood up and said: "Then I would play; when a famous conductor visits I'd be in the orchestra; I'd be doing something that I enjoyed; I wouldn't feel I had become idle and useless, that…" Alaleh wiped a tear from her cheek and fell silent.

Farhad took her hand and said: "This is exactly what I told you, but you put your instrument away and decided you didn't want to have anything to do with it; and that was because…" Alaleh said angrily: "Yes, because the faculty was closed; because I got married; because I had a baby; because the missiles kept coming". Then she looked Farhad in the eye and tried to control herself. She smiled and said: "No, it wasn't because of you and Shaghayegh...but with the sound of bullets, missiles, military marches, the air-raid sirens and I don't know how many thousands of other miseries, it seemed to me frivolous to play music; but I realise now that I made a mistake; I made a mistake; I never took myself seriously...never..."

Shaghayegh, who was getting worried, came out of her room and went to the bathroom. Silence filled the room for a few seconds. Shaghayegh came out of the bathroom and said: "The hand of the clock is on the last quarter, it must be time for an argument," and went into the kitchen. Farhad said: "Anyway, tell me, what made you go to the rehearsal? You never go there". Alaleh thought: "He always goes to the heart of the matter. It's almost impossible to pull the wool over his eyes". She sighed, and said: "No reason really, one of my old fellow students who went to France to study after graduating is coming back to conduct some performances; and as a matter of fact I went to see how everything was. I have to coordinate his programme". Farhad breathed long and deeply, and asked: "What's his name?" Alaleh paused, then in the most neutral tone that she could muster said: "Hormoz Shadan".

"Hormoz?" Farhad asked in amazement.

Alaleh said: "Yes".

Farhad smirked and said: "So you picked up your instrument again as a present for Maestro Shadan".

Shaghayegh came out of the kitchen carrying the tea tray. Alaleh breathed a sigh of relief; she had told him. Farhad turned on the TV and looked at the screen. Shaghayegh was observing him sidelong. No, he didn't seem to be angry. Once more Alaleh lay down on the sofa and Shaghayegh didn't go back to her room. She knew very well how much those two loved each other, but just for a second she had been worried. Now that she saw they were calm she was consumed with curiosity. She wanted to ask Alaleh at the first opportunity who Hormoz Shadan was. It seemed strange to her that her mother had retrieved her instrument from the store room; and now she wanted to know what kind of influence this Hormoz Shadan had on her mother, so that his coming had changed her mood. Her young nose smelt love and affection in this story and she was getting increasingly curious. She felt she loved her mother even more because they were of the same sex. But now she must change the subject; she put the little dish of sugar lumps in front of Alaleh and said: "Mum, tomorrow I have to go to Mehri's house because it's her birthday; can I borrow your pink blouse?" Alaleh smiled at her and said: "Of course".

Shaghayegh took her mother's hand and said: "Let's go and see if it fits me," and forced her to follow. Farhad understood why Shaghayegh had taken Alaleh and thought: "What made her so anxious? Is it because Hormoz is coming? How did I behave? Where did Shaghayegh learn to be so crafty? Alaleh, no doubt, would say from her aunts." And since Farhad couldn't find a satisfactory answer he laughed and stood up to join them. Shaghayegh, looking very pretty in her mother's blouse, kissed Alaleh on the cheek and went to her own room.

Farhad went to the bathroom. Alaleh pulled off the bedspread and threw herself on the bed. In the bathroom, as he cleaned his teeth, Farhad thought: "I've lost my hair, my front teeth are crowned, but fortunately they're hidden by my moustache. I'm twenty kilos overweight, but I don't see why I shouldn't be a match for the maestro; he must have changed a lot too since he was nineteen. I've never liked the taste of this toothpaste and I don't know why Alaleh insists on buying it. Alaleh still loves me as she did in those days. I'm sure of it, because she nearly scratched Mrs. Sadri's eyes out when we were at Abbas's house. She didn't like it at all when Mrs. Sadri talked to me. Anyway, anyone could have liked someone when they were young; I kind of liked our neighbour's daughter, Pari. Although she was very plump; but then I wasn't in love with anybody until Alaleh came along. Now she's definitely wondering how she should behave; I wish I could tell her I trust her and I understand her; but I'm afraid deep down I'm a little bit worried. Is it possible that when she meets the maestro her love will be reborn? No, these front teeth are quite clean; I wish I had more hair. Oh, that Mr. Safri with his dyed hair; the boys say he and his father-in-law use the same hair dye. I've brushed my teeth so much the enamel has come off. I must buy a few new shirts and a more modern pair of glasses. These frames make me look very old. Shaghayegh has become very crafty. Alaleh still looks more beautiful when she's playing; and yet..."

Alaleh put her hands under her head and thought: "I said it at last. I was afraid he would react badly; I know he trusts me, but no one knows about other people's feelings. I wish I was as certain as he is. I don't know what he looks like now; surely like Farhad he has put on weight and lost his hair. By God, I hope his character hasn't changed. What if he has become like a foreigner? It would be very interesting for Shaghayegh to see him. I don't know what she's thinking. Perhaps she thinks I was frivolous and flighty. But no..., girls these days are much more open-minded than we were. I wish I hadn't got so old. I must have my hair done and maybe dye it; what colour? What colour...?"

Shaghayegh had opened her course book and was reading, but she kept getting distracted. Staring at the text she thought: "How interesting; a friend of her youth; when will I fall in love? I didn't mind Mansoor, but he was a bit spoiled. So Alaleh too had loved someone else in the past; what about dad? He too must have liked one or two girls. How fantastic it would be if I could see all of them. Sometimes when Grandma gets annoyed with dad she tells me: "You don't know how many suitors your mother had." But Alaleh says she didn't have many boyfriends; I wouldn't marry someone I didn't choose; I'm sure Alaleh is now very anxious; anxious about what? Damn these studies. What will we ever remember of it? Farhad is behaving like someone who's not at all jealous. I want to get married when I'm twenty-two. Is it possible to marry your first love? I must tell Alaleh to pay more attention to her appearance. I don't want her looking old and tired when she meets her friend. He must understand that she's quite happy with us. It's interesting that I'm feeling jealous towards her. I feel protective of our family's honour. Like those thugs in the old films who wear those black hats. I'll be careful and won't let the arrival of a friend affect our lives. I wish he wouldn't come at all; but no, if he wasn't coming Alaleh wouldn't play her instrument and I'm sure she needs to do this; we must go and get her some contact lenses. Sometimes she looks very plain...I must look after her a bit more. Sometimes I think I should have been her mother...it's so simple...it's so nice..."

The rehearsals were progressing well under one of the conductors. All the arrangements had been made and everything seemed fine, apart from Alaleh's agitated mind. Her mind was working constantly at a crazy speed, jumping from one thought to another: "What is Farhad thinking? How would Shaghayegh react? Could she go to the airport? What to say to the others? Does she look too old? She could play for him one evening. It would be better if she didn't wear glasses. How will she feel when she sees him? Will she blush? Will she recognise him? Will the programmes go smoothly? Please let there not be any problems. Which manteau should she wear to the airport? Will she be able to talk to him at last? Will she find out how he felt about her? Will Farhad like Hormoz? Has Shaghayegh fallen in love yet? If one of Farhad's old friends, for instance a female friend, was coming from abroad what would she do? Could she tolerate her? Does Hormoz love his wife? Had he really loved her, or did he think of her just like all the others?"

All of these thoughts were pounding her head like a hammer. As the day of his arrival came closer, the speed and intensity of the hammering increased. She had very little appetite. She was anxious all the time and there was just one sentence which kept repeating in her head: "I only want to know, that's all". They had never been able to speak frankly to each other, and it seemed now as if Alaleh wanted to remember her former self through Hormoz's memories.

After a month Alaleh gradually emerged from her state of confusion and distraction. Everything seemed to be in order and Farhad didn't mention anything, while Shaghayegh seemed to be waiting for something. An expectation mixed with sympathy; little by little excitement would replace anxiety. For more than a month she had convinced herself that Hormoz's return would be a simple matter, the same as when her other friends had come back, a welcome, a little chat and then goodbye; a few more memories to be added to the memories of twenty years ago. Exactly like the pearl beads of a necklace taking their place one by one as the string goes through them until there is no more space and the necklace has been completed. All she has to do is play it safe until it is all over. She must prepare all her masks so her face would not betray her. When everybody else is so thoughtful and gets on calmly with every situation why shouldn't she be wise? But no matter however hard she tried it was impossible, her masks would fall and break and wisdom would leave her head. She felt she still owed Farhad an explanation.

There were still forty days to go before Hormoz's arrival when one evening, as she sat cross-legged on the settee, she snatched the newspaper from Farhad and stared directly into his eyes. Farhad was a first taken aback and then started to look worried. He knew this kind of mood of Alaleh's very well: this meant she wanted to talk to him about something and that it was very important to her. So in order to show his readiness, he too sat cross-legged on the settee opposite her and waited. But Alaleh frowned and said: "Look Farhad, stop fooling around; I want to talk to you about something very important." Farhad's expression became serious and he said: "I'm listening." Alaleh pulled on her necklace and said: "Look, I wanted you to know something; Hormoz's coming is the coming an old friend, that is all, and I am now a forty-year-old woman who is married and has a daughter and I look at him only as a friend, that is all." Farhad laughed and thought: "She doesn't even believe what she is saying" but he said: "I too want you to know something: that the fact of Hormoz's coming is the coming of an old friend and that you are now a forty-year-old woman who has a husband and a daughter, that is all. And also it would help if you paid more attention to your hair because it looks quite messy and then don't worry about anything: I am not a jealous man at all; that is all." And then he held her hands. Alaleh pulled her hands away from his and thought: "Then surely he doesn't really love me much, otherwise..."

Farhad took hold of her hands again and said: "I trust you so much; I love you so much; I trust you so much that ..."

Alaleh got up and laughed and said: "But I don't trust you at all; if ever an old friend of yours happens to show herself I will scratch her eyes out with my own nails."

Farhad roared with laughter and said: "This is what you call a real woman."

After that night Alaleh felt calmer. Now deep down she felt like teasing Farhad; didn't he claim not to be jealous? They will see about that. She resumed her work with a new impetus; she booked the plane ticket and sent it. She checked everything and attended all the rehearsals. Now there was a marked reduction in her dislike of Mrs. Saghafi's face. Every day after work when she got home in the late afternoon she would practise the piece he was playing and gradually she began to believe that she played it even better than her.

One morning a few days later she was sitting at her desk watching the first falling of the snow and drinking tea when the phone rang. Suddenly her heart sank. She was, once again, thinking about Hormoz's coming and at such moments her heart would start pounding, like that of a naughty child who had been caught with the box of sweets. It was Mrs. Shirazi. Her voice sounded terribly hoarse. She wanted Alaleh to inform the bosses of her absence and get her a sick note confirming a medical emergency break for her. Alaleh asked her if she needed anything and Mrs. Shirazi said no, when the snow stopped she would go out shopping herself.

It was around ten o'clock that Alaleh finished what she had to do for the day; she looked at Mrs. Shirazi's desk to see if there was anything that couldn't wait and needed to be done so she could do it; but there wasn't. She filled in Mrs. Shirazi's emergency medical certificate and took it to their manager's office, then decided to pop in and have a look at the rehearsal. She sat in her usual place and listened to the music. It was the first movement of a symphony she knew very well; she sat back and closed her eyes. Did he ever remember her? If he came and saw her there what would he say? She listened again. What if the players did not perform well? If... Suddenly the sound of a cello was heard loud and clear and Alaleh felt as she was hearing nails on a blackboard. She sat up straight and opened her eyes. Then she bent and looked carefully at Mrs. Saghafi. She was playing out of tune; at least three notes were played out of tune, Alaleh was absolutely sure of that. Suddenly she saw a glimmer of hope; for a few seconds her whole being was suffused with happiness, but after a few seconds her happiness subsided and she laughed at herself and her folly. It would be impossible for her to play instead of Mrs. Saghafi. But the delight and the pleasure of the thought were too great to be so easily eroded. She got up and went out. Did Mrs Saghafi really play that badly or had she just become very sensitive about it? What the hell does this Mrs. Saghafi want from her anyway? Wasn't it possible to choose someone else instead of her? Alaleh returned to her room and sat down, feeling the lack of Mrs. Shirazi. She was desperate to chat to someone; someone as close to her as Mrs. Shirazi; someone who knew her workplace and the people who worked there. Suddenly she missed her terribly. She picked up her bag and told the secretary there was something she urgently needed to do and that she would be back in two hours.

She rang Mrs. Shirazi's doorbell. At first there was no answer. Alaleh thought: "Poor thing, how lonely she must be." And then she saw Mrs. Shirazi with dishevelled hair looking out of the window and on seeing Alaleh she screamed and disappeared from sight. It took a minute or two before the door was buzzed open and Alaleh pushed it with her knee. She changed the bags she was carrying from one hand to the other and went towards the stairs. She imagined Mrs. Shirazi hastily rushing around, making the bed, brushing her hair and putting on a dressing gown over her nightdress. When she reached the door to the apartment, she pushed it open with her foot and entered the hall. She was shocked. Everywhere was shining with cleanliness and everything seemed to be where it was meant to be. She had given Mrs Shirazi a lift a few times but had been come up to her apartment. She stood in the hall and waited. Mrs. Shirazi came out of her bedroom; she was wearing a beautiful clean casual dress and was busy putting a pin in her hair; like this, she looked younger. Her greying hair gave her a particular air of gravity and she didn't look at all the kind who could talk incessantly for half an hour about a lipstick or the price of a kilo of meat, or be capable of laughing very loudly. Mrs. Shirazi took the bags from her and said: "Oh, thank you, you shouldn't have done this; it is so kind of you. Why did you put yourself to so much trouble? Oh God, I am so embarrassed about all this." Alaleh took off her manteau and headscarf and said: "Well I still don't know if I have done the right thing or not?" Mrs. Shirazi said: "Oh, how very embarrassing." Alaleh followed Mrs. Shirazi into the kitchen. She sat on the only chair at a small table and looked at the doors and the walls, while listening all the time to Mrs. Shirazi's various expressions of gratitude. The kitchen units were so clean that they were shining. The stovetop was sparkling and there were many different coloured handmade and crocheted kitchen cloths hanging from the hooks on the wall. Here and there were flower pots with dried flowers and different coloured terracotta containers for sugar, sugar lumps and tea, as well as small jars of jams and pickles which all together created a warm and happy atmosphere. Mrs Shirazi put a glass of tea in front of her and said: "Didn't they ask why I hadn't turned up?" Alaleh laughed and said: "You are sick; but you don't look all that sick to me." Mrs. Shirazi wiped her hands and said: "Oh yes; when I got up in the morning I had lost my voice; then I took two cold tablets and I had a bit of temperature too, but I'm better now." Alaleh took a sip of her tea and said: "Rest for two or three days till you have completely recovered." Mrs. Shirazi took a stool from under the table; she sat opposite Alaleh and asked her: "But how come you decided to come here?" Alaleh wanted to say: "I needed to talk to someone" or "I felt sorry for your loneliness," but instead she said: "No reason, I just wanted to buy a few essentials so you wouldn't have to go out." Mrs. Shirazi looked at her affectionately and said: "You have done a wonderful thing; I don't know how to thank you." Alaleh felt embarrassed. She got up hurriedly and said: "Now I am going to make you some chicken soup; quickly, urgently and instantly." Mrs. Shirazi stood up and said: "I'll make it myself." But Alaleh who was now in a good mood said: "Just sit and don't move; I'll prepare the soup and while I do I'll tell you a funny story to make you laugh a bit." Watching the movement of her hands Mrs. Shirazi said: "You look much younger and much more beautiful without the headscarf." Alaleh blushed and said: "If only you knew how much I need this compliment," and laughed a little hysterically. Then while washing the chicken she said: "Did you know that I have been going to watch the rehearsals over the past few days?" Mrs. Shirazi looked surprised and said:

"Seriously? But you said you hated dark and enclosed places." Alaleh plucked the last feather from the chicken and said: "Well, I didn't mean what I said. Now that someone is coming from abroad I'll have to be more careful and attentive." Mrs. Shirazi smiled and said: "You seem to be making a big fuss over this, what is going on?" Alaleh put the chicken in a basket and said: "Well, Shadan was at university with me so I would like his concert to go smoothly." Mrs. Shirazi got up; she removed the chicken from the basket and placed it on the chopping board and cut one of the thighs off and said: "If I asked you something would you give me an honest answer?" Alaleh said "Yes, well…" She was cutting the onion and crying as a result. Mrs. Shirazi cut off the other thigh and said: "Was there something going on between you and this Shadan?" Alaleh sniffed and said: "Oh, absolutely not; in those days I wasn't into such things, and anyway in those days he had hundreds of girlfriends." She wiped her tears and thought: "It was pointless coming here, once again I have been so stupid." Mrs. Shirazi looked at her and when she saw the tears in her eyes she believed her. Alaleh wiped her eyes with the end of her sleeve and wanted to change the subject so she said: "But the funny thing I was going to say is that there is a woman who plays the cello in the orchestra who looks like a cat; believe me: short, plump and with green eyes." Mrs. Shirazi laughed and said: "Well that's funny, to have a cat playing the cello." Alaleh scattered the chopped onion over the chicken and said: "Believe me she can't reach the upper part of the instrument." Mrs. Shirazi took a box of baklava from the fridge and said: "But you never told me why you gave up playing." Alaleh turned red and whispered: "Forget about it, I was talking about the woman; her name is Saghafi and she was one of those audacious characters at university; she wasn't talented but instead she was arrogant and full of herself and still you can't imagine how badly she plays."

Mrs. Shirazi sniggered and said: "I know her; she belongs to the third-raters and Mr. Kangarani doesn't like her at all but Mr. Parvizi is looking after her. Anyway there is nothing to be done now unless she has an accident." And she laughed.

Alaleh looked at her not too pleased, thinking that Mrs Shirazi knew everything and was playing a game with her; she didn't say anything else; she finished her tea and got up and adjusting her scarf said: "Well, I must really get going now; if you need anything just give me a call." At the door Mrs. Shirazi got hold of her hands and said: "I'll never forget your kindness." But Alaleh was pissed off; pissed off with herself for being so rash and doing things without thinking properly about the consequences.

About twenty days before Hormoz's arrival, one evening after dinner Shaghayegh said: "Alaleh, don't you think you had better get some contact lenses because these glasses make you look old." Alaleh laughed but didn't say anything. She thought to herself: she is mocking me too. And Farhad went on: "Apart from anything else, glasses somehow distort the expressions in one's eyes and your eyes are the only feature of your face that is not too bad." Alaleh frowned and said: "Are you two colluding to make fun of me, hey?" Shaghayegh said: "What makes you think that? Dad and I love you so much that we always want to see you looking beautiful and in good form." Alaleh threw a cushion at her and said: "Really, the two of you are made of the same stuff." Farhad coughed mockingly and said: "No, I'm serious; these days everybody wears lenses." Alaleh took her glasses off and cleaned them. Shaghayegh continued: "I swear to God you look much nicer without glasses." Alaleh shrugged her shoulders. Shaghayegh crossed her eyes and said: "Well, you keep on doing this, it's no wonder dad is eying other women." Alaleh put her glasses back on and muttered:

"He wouldn't dare." Shaghayegh went and sat down next to her mother; she got as close to her as possible and said affectionately: "I'm serious; you must have your hair done, buy lenses and a few new clothes." Alaleh stopped frowning and deep down felt quite happy. She wanted to make some changes to her appearance but she preferred the suggestion to come from them. Farhad, who knew that Alaleh was practising during the day when they were out, said: "You can also do your nails..." Shaghayegh held her mother's hands, looked at her nails and said: "No, her hands are beautiful as they are; I'll use the emery board a little to smooth them and then put some pale nail varnish on them; that would be enough; these hands are the hands of a musician." And she winked mischievously at Farhad. Alaleh looked at the two of them and thought: "They are in total harmony" and was agitated because she didn't know how they felt and she was not even sure about how she felt herself. Now everybody was teasing her: Shaghayegh, Mrs. Shirazi and even her mother and her aunts. It seemed as if the coming of Hormoz had taken everybody back to their youths. They all were waiting eagerly for his arrival.

As he looked at her Farhad thought: "She is thinking; whenever she stares at something like that it means something is seriously occupying her mind, she is confused; she doesn't know that if I could do something to prevent her from seeing him I would definitely do it. I keep telling myself I shouldn't worry, but things can get complicated. If I just face the situation normally it will pass quickly and everything will be back to normal." Farhad took a sugar lump from the dish and threw it at Alaleh. Alaleh looked at him in confusion. Farhad said: "By the way, what do you think about tinted lenses?" and laughed loudly.

Alaleh got up and went into the bedroom. She felt like being by herself. Shaghayegh brought her dad some tea; she sat down opposite him and put her hands under her chin and stared at him. Farhad looked at her and said: "Haven't you seen me before?" Shaghayegh pushed her hair behind her ears and said: "Don't you honestly feel a little bit jealous?" Farhad smiled and said: "Well, a little, but this is something that could happen to anybody and we mustn't make too much fuss about it." Shaghayegh said: "But if after seeing him again..." Farhad cut her off in the middle of her sentence and said: "Alaleh loves you and me more than anything else in the world; I am absolutely certain of that; what has disturbed her is not just the coming of Hormoz; it is that she thinks she is getting old and the fact that she has wasted he life and hasn't achieved what she wanted to achieve; and then she is scared, very scared of her own reactions.

And we must help her to go through this period as easily as possible; and by the way, do you know that your mum is the best woman in the world?" Shaghayegh pouted and said in a childish voice: "The way you two praise each other, it's enough to make anyone jealous." Then she hit her dad on the knee very hard and laughed.

The arrival of Hormoz was getting nearer and nearer with every day that passed, and the closer the date came the more composed Alaleh felt. The arrangements relating to the concert were proceeding smoothly and alongside her work she continued to practise two hours a day. She now felt very comfortable in putting aside anything which came between her and her practice; every day she would start on time and her confidence increased as she improved. And it was now Shaghayegh who seemed worried and anxious. Something was happening and she wished she could be an important part of it. She felt she must, somehow, look after her mother and at the same time she was extremely curious about Hormoz while feeling a little scared of him. But she didn't know what to do and was waiting for an opportunity to have a straight talk with Alaleh and because she had never done this she was apprehensive about it. As much as it was easy for her to talk to her dad she found it difficult to talk to her mum. She felt as if a thin but strong curtain separated her from her mother. She was afraid her mother would see her as being too young to talk to about all of her problems. But the opportunity presented itself, because Farhad was going to be away on a business trip for a couple of days and they would be alone together.

The first day, when Shaghayegh got home in the late afternoon she found her mother sitting in front of the dressing table mirror and playing the cello. She greeted her quietly and lay on the bed to listen. This was the first time she had enjoyed classical music. She lay on her side in order to watch her mother and suddenly it seemed to her that they were far apart. She didn't know how long it was before her mother put her bow down and stood up. Shaghayegh asked: "What was the piece?" Alaleh smiled when she saw her expression and said: "Adagio by Albinoni." Shaghayegh touched her hair and said: "It was beautiful, but you were even more beautiful. By the way, did you know that when you are playing you look very different?" She sat up on the bed and said: "If I were you I would take my instrument with me wherever I went." Alaleh was overcome with happiness. She felt a surge of love for her daughter and her face turned as red as a beetroot. She took

Shaghayegh round the waist, kissed her and said: "Shall we have fried eggs or spinach omelette?" She wanted to change the subject. Shaghayegh kissed her back and said: "Spinach omelette" and together they went into the kitchen. Alaleh took a bunch of frozen spinach from the freezer and dropped it into the frying pan and poured some oil over it. Shaghayegh said: "I think light brown suits you."

At bedtime they said goodnight to each other and each went to her own bedroom. Alaleh picked up the novel she had been reading and began to read; she read but she didn't understand anything. She was thinking about Shaghayegh. She knew that so far she had not tried very hard to establish a close relationship with her daughter; of course she did everything for her but she knew that between her and Farhad, the one she relied on more was Farhad. Until now she had looked at their relationship with a kind of indifference. She knew Farhad loved his daughter very much and in a way she had just kept out of the way. But now she felt that to get to know Shaghayegh some changes were taking place inside her and these changes made it easier to enter Shaghayegh's world; a world that belonged to her and Shaghayegh and that Farhad could not enter. Now she looked at her as a woman and it seemed to her that it was time for her to acknowledge the fact that her daughter was a woman and establish a new kind of relationship, apart from the mother-daughter relationship; a kind of intimacy that Farhad was not able to give her. She wanted to know what Shaghayegh thought about Hormoz and whether she had ever fallen in love. She had noticed that sometimes Shaghayegh had paid more attention to some people than to others, but they had never talked about it.

She was still on the same page when the door opened and Shaghayegh appeared at the door in her long white nightdress, carrying a pillow under her arm. Alaleh sat up and smiled at her and it occurred to her that: "Like her father, she anticipates situations better than I do and always gets there first." Shaghayegh said: "I couldn't sleep". Alaleh put her book down on the bedside table, pulled back the corner of the duvet and said: "Please, come in." Shaghayegh, who hadn't been sure of how her mother would receive her, was beside herself with joy; she jumped onto the bed and put her arms round her mother's neck. Alaleh held her tight and kissed her hair and felt her grown-up girl was now a small woman with whom she could become very intimate. She regretted that they had not reached this point earlier and promised herself that from now on she would do everything to understand her daughter, her younger sister, her friend and perhaps some time in the future her mother! Wasn't it true that old people became like children and needed the motherly love of their own children?

They lay their heads on one pillow and held hands. Shaghayegh's heart was pounding and she felt like squeezing her mother so hard that she would scream. Alaleh asked: "Well, why couldn't you go to sleep?" Shaghayegh smiled mischievously and said: "If I ask you something, will you do it for me?" Alaleh said: "Like what for example?" Shaghayegh said: "I won't say, you must promise first." Alaleh guessed what she wanted to hear and this was exactly what she herself wanted. She caressed her daughter's hair and said: "I promise." Shaghayegh smiled and said: "You must tell me everything." Alaleh, disconcerted by so much bluntness, asked: "What is it you want me to tell you?" Shaghayegh messed her mother's hair so it covered her forehead and said: "Don't pretend you don't know what I'm talking about; I'm grown up now." Alaleh pulled back the hair from her forehead and stared at her. Shaghayegh noticed and said: "Farhad has told me a little bit about Hormoz." Alaleh gave a short scream and said: "What? What has he said?" Shaghayegh laughed; now she was holding the trump card. She sat up on the bed and said: "Don't panic; a while ago he was talking to me and telling me that young people fall in love at some point in their lives but the whole of your life does not depend on that first love. Usually people don't marry their first love; you might not even talk to your first love; but it is a beautiful feeling which sweetens your memories."

Alaleh was confused; she didn't know if should be happy about what Farhad had done or not. Suddenly she remembered the main question and asked: "And what did he say about Hormoz Shadan?" Shaghayegh sat with her arms crossed across her chest and said: "Give me a hundred Tomans and I'll tell you..." Alaleh was angry but tried to keep her composure; she pinched her daughter's leg and said laughing: "For mummy's sake, what did he say?" Shaghayegh lay back on the bed; she rested her head on her hands and said: "Farhad said you had fallen in love two and a half times and he, himself, three times." Looking surprised Alaleh asked: "Three times?" Shaghayegh said: "If you want to know about him you must pay two hundred Tomans." Alaleh, who was now quite impatient, said pleadingly: "Well then, tell me." Shaghayegh stroked her mother's hair a little and said: "Never forget that I am a girl who can keep secrets." Alaleh moved her pillow on its spot and said: "No, what did he say about Hormoz?

Because I know he has lied about having fallen in love three times!" Shaghayegh raised her eyebrows and said: "How do you know; Farhad is still a very handsome man; he is pretty popular amongst the students in my faculty." Once more Alaleh pinched her leg and said: "Well, well; stop making so much fuss about your father; now tell me: what did he say about Hormoz?" Shaghayegh stared at the ceiling and said: "First you talk about it and then I will." Alaleh bent over her daughter's face and said: "If I asked you one thing will you tell me the truth?" Shaghayegh said: "If you take me to the airport." Alaleh said: "Who wants to go to the airport? Now tell me, isn't Farhad angry about all of this business?" Shaghayegh looked at her mischievously and said: "Oh no, in his opinion all of this is quite normal; after all he too had been in love before." Alaleh gently pulled at her hair and said: "Damn it, you have taken after your father!" Shaghayegh laughed and embraced her mother and said: "And that is why I love you, now come on and tell me."

Alaleh was feeling relieved. The fact that Farhad had talked to Shaghayegh about it meant he had come to terms with it. Alaleh turned towards Shaghayegh and pointed at a few stars which could be seen shining through the window and said: "Do you see those stars in the sky?"

Shaghayegh, sounding a bit displeased, said: "Well, yes what about them?"

- How do they look when you keep staring at them?
- They twinkle.
- No, they are not twinkling, they are laughing.

Surprised by her mother's answer Shaghayegh asked:

- Laughing?
- Yes, the stars are laughing at all the men and women who had, at one time, been in love and all those men and women look at the sky every night, looking to find their own stars, and smile at them surreptitiously.
- What about me, do I have a star?

Alaleh caressed her head and said:

- You will have one day, my love; you too will one day. Of course, provided you haven't had one so far. These stars are the loves that young people experience. And you, when you look at the stars you know that somewhere, somewhere in the world there is someone whose heart warms up when that person is thinking about you.

Shaghayegh touched her mother's necklace and said: "This star hanging from your neck, did Farhad buy this for you for the same reason?"

Alaleh sighed and said: "The last love is the one you wear round your neck; a star that you can't see unless you look into the mirror: just like your eyes. But when you touch it you see a blue halo round your fingers and your whole being comes to life."

Shaghayegh laughed and said: "You should have become a poet."

- Farhad bought me this star when we were engaged and I have never taken it off since.

Shaghayegh looked at the tip of her fingers and stared at the sky. Then she sighed and said:

- You don't love Hormoz any more?
- I do love him, just like a star. I know he is dear to me because he carries a lot with him: youth, happiness during the university years, music and thousand other things that all have finished and gone.
- Then why didn't you marry each other?
- You never marry the stars.

Shaghayegh frowned and said:

- For God's sake, get away from the stars; why didn't you marry each other?

Alaleh said:

- We were too young; our paths were different.

And then she laughed loudly and continued:

- Well, apart from that Hormoz had a string of stars.

Shaghayegh sat up again; she knew she could ask her mother everything she wanted to.

And she did:
- Was he handsome?
- Not bad looking; he was interesting; he talked big talk and he played the piano very well.
- If I asked you a question would you answer me truthfully?
- Of course.
- Would you now prefer to be married to Hormoz instead of Farhad?

Alaleh thought a little and then said:
- To be honest, no. Because we would be a couple of people who lived in dreams and away from reality. We were too similar to be able to live together. I needed someone I could lean on, and your father is the best support in the world.

Shaghayegh laughed and said:
- Wait till he gets here, I'll tell him.

Alaleh arranged the duvet over her and said:
- If you see me being a little agitated these days it is not my fault; it is the fault of that nineteen-year-old Alaleh who comes to see this forty-year-old Alaleh and keeps jumping about and moving here and there. Now time to go to sleep.

And she switched off the light.

Shaghayegh held her mother's arm and fell asleep very quickly but Alaleh was thinking about their conversation for another hour.

The following day Alaleh arrived at work a little later than usual. Mrs. Shirazi was sitting behind her desk and looked busy. On seeing Alaleh she raised her head and, imitating a character on a TV programme, said: "Greetings to you." Alaleh laughed and said: "It has become universal now." Mrs. Shirazi said: "Because it is very funny. Well how is her ladyship? It seems that today, touch wood, she is on good form."

Alaleh looked at her a little surprised and said: "But I am always on good form." Mrs. Shirazi imitated her: "I am always on good form, of course; who are you kidding? For one or two weeks now you have been behaving as if you don't even know me; all your attention is focused on that person who is coming from Paris; you have even photocopied the music yourself and handed it out to the musicians. And then when you have seen that everything is going smoothly you sit here and stare at the window, the light; in short you just stare at everything. Everything except poor me; no doubt in a few days when he comes you won't even bother to come to the office. For God's sake, I'm bored; say something, talk, because my teeth are getting rusty because I haven't used my mouth."

Since the day she had visited Mrs. Shirazi at her apartment and got upset, Alaleh had been a bit non-committal without meaning to; now she realised that she might have gone too far. She put her bag on the desk and said: "Forgive me, you're right; maybe I was too wrapped up in my work; but now I'm ready and can give you both my ears."

Mrs. Shirazi narrowed her eyes and said: "I'll tell you something." And Alaleh said nonchalantly: "Tell me." Mrs. Shirazi said very quietly: "Recently you have been talking to yourself." Looking worried, Alaleh asked: "What do I say?"

Mrs. Shirazi laughed mischievously and said: "Oh nothing, don't worry about it."

Alaleh knew that Mrs. Shirazi would never miss an opportunity to gather information, so she decided to change the subject and said: "In your view, if I were to dye my hair, what colour would suit me?"

Mrs. Shirazi said: "Well, well, how very strange that her ladyship has suddenly remembered her hair."

Alaleh was thinking that it was impossible to get away easily from Mrs. Shirazi, so she said: "No, I was only joking... To tell you the truth it's Shaghayegh who is insisting on it; she seems to be looking for a younger mother." Mrs. Shirazi rummaged through the letters on her desk and said: "I think light brown with blonde highlights would make you look amazing." Alaleh laughed and said: "Blonde highlights? I don't think so; don't you think it would make me irresistible?"

Mrs. Shirazi shrugged and said while looking for a particular letter: "If I had a husband like Farhad I would dye my hair a different colour every day." Alaleh opened her folder and said: "Seriously, you have gone crazy" and she began to work.

It was around midday when Shaghayegh phoned her and said she would see her at two in front of the hairdresser's. Alaleh put the receiver down and, not knowing what to do, stared at Mrs. Shirazi.

Mrs. Shirazi said: "What's the matter?" Alaleh pulled her scarf down and said: "Nothing, my daughter's made an appointment for me at the hairdresser's… What should I say when I get there?"

Mrs. Shirazi said: "Nothing, just say light brown with blonde highlights; and of course it's always possible that Shaghayegh has already decided. It's clear that this girl is turning into a real lady: very fashionable and with good taste, unlike her mother who seems to be uninterested and frumpy; but in any case dark red is not bad either." Alaleh was fed up now so she got up and went to the bathroom. She removed her scarf and looked at herself in the mirror. When she returned to her office she had already made up her mind.

When she entered the hairdresser's she felt like a little girl whose mother had taken her by the hand and brought her there by force. She sat on the chair; a girl came and put a gown over her head and then a middle-aged lady approached her holding a pair of scissors. Alaleh looked at Shaghayegh in desperation. Shaghayegh said: "Just a little bit to tidy it up," and then without waiting for a reply she said to the hairdresser: "Cut it short, please."

Alaleh, very surprised, looked at her again. Shaghayegh said: "It means cutting it to your ears or even shorter if you prefer." Alaleh, who was feeling worried, asked: "You mean short, short?" Shaghayegh said: "No, don't worry, only up to the ears: it's fashionable, and apart from anything else it is also artistic," and laughed. Alaleh didn't say anything after that; she felt she was quite powerless amongst all those people who knew what they were doing. The hairdresser began to work. When she cut the first bit of her hair Alaleh sighed, but when the hairdresser gradually reached the front and she saw her face she felt she was looking younger and younger. Alaleh's smile when it was finished made Shaghayegh very happy. Then she pointed at another chair and said: "Now here." Alaleh picked up her bag and went and sat on the chair. She hadn't yet sat down or said anything when a girl arrived carrying a bowl of hair dye and a brush. Trying not to shout Alaleh called: "Shaghayegh". Shaghayegh put her hand on her shoulder and said: "It is a shade lighter than your own hair; only a shade lighter." Alaleh sighed again and accepted her fate and while she was looking at her ridiculous face in the mirror she thought about this first meeting after so many years. She was still deep in her thoughts when they helped her move and took her to another room. They took away the towel from her face and washed her hair. She didn't recognise herself. She looked at least eight years younger and Shaghayegh was beside herself with joy. Now they both wanted to see Farhad's reaction.

When the doorbell went later in the afternoon, Shaghayegh went to the window and said: "He's here," and went to open the door. Alaleh touched and arranged her hair for the last time and took her glasses off and retreated a little bit and straightened the creases of her shirt. Wearing that blue shirt and those denim trousers she looked a completely different person. She looked at the room once more; everything looked perfect; the sunflowers had made the atmosphere of the room warm and the fruit bowl piled up with colourful fruit and the cake dishes on the table all spoke of a pending sweet and romantic event. Two knocks on the apartment door and Shaghayegh opened it. Farhad kissed his daughter and put down everything he was carrying. He then raised his head and shouted: "Alaleh". Alaleh came out of the room trying to walk like a model on a catwalk and said: "Greetings". Farhad didn't answer and looked at her in amazement; then he smiled and said: "Is that you or have they exchanged you for someone else?"

At last the day Farhad was due to go away arrived and he left, leaving the car for them. Both Alaleh and Shaghayegh were very agitated. As they were getting into the car, Shaghayegh looked at her mother for the last time. Without her glasses and just a little makeup she looked at least ten years younger and, in her coat and the navy blue headscarf with a cherry pattern, she looked stunning. Shaghayegh frowned and said: "Like this, nobody will pay any attention to me!" She held the car door open for her and went and sat behind the wheel. She turned the engine on and said: "The lenses aren't hurting you, are they?" Alaleh laughed nervously and said: "Right now I want to take them out and throw them out of the window."

- You get used to them. Like this he will think I am your sister.

Alaleh was fiddling with the strap of her handbag and said: "Pay attention to your driving; just don't have an accident."

Shaghayegh realised that she should not tease her mother any more. Together and in silence they watched the lights of the oncoming cars. Alaleh didn't have a clue how she should behave when she saw him. She knew that his family would all be there to welcome him so she was anxious about how he would behave towards her and Shaghayegh. She felt her heart was beating faster than usual. She put her hand on her heart and said: "It would be funny if he didn't recognise me at all; or like foreigners nodded his head and said he was grateful I had come to the airport." Shaghayegh squeezed her hand and said: "I am pretty sure he would be as excited as you are when he sees you." Alaleh rearranged her headscarf and said: "And I am pretty sure he wouldn't be like me."

Alaleh was well aware that the passing of years and going through life and having had different experiences had changed the two of them and that their feelings were somehow very different. Now she was expecting to see the extent of these changes. She knew that inside the memory frame of the other each had assumed a different shape and appearance, and thought how she wished the frame in which her memory had been kept was made of china: white with blue patterns of flowers. She noticed that Shaghayegh was once again stealthily watching her. She pulled down her headscarf a little and said: "For God's sake don't keep looking at me, it makes me nervous." Shaghayegh stopped at a red light and said: "I hope I will have a star when I am your age, a smiling star; a star round my neck that would make the tip of my fingers blue."

Once again they were both quiet. When at last Shaghayegh parked the car in the airport car park she remembered her dad's last sentence. He had said: "This is just a game that might bring Alaleh back to life and happiness and for her sake we must go along playing the game." Shaghayegh locked the car and whispered to herself: "What an exciting game!"

Alaleh glared at her and waited till Shaghayegh came to her and then the two of them started walking together towards the airport's waiting lounge. Of the two, the one who seemed to be more excited about the meeting was Shaghayegh, because by now Alaleh wasn't sure if she had done the right thing by coming to the airport. A force was pulling her towards the airport lounge and another force was holding her back. And in all of this only Shaghayegh seemed to be the most reliable support so she held her arm and closed her eyes and allowed her daughter to lead her on. She hoped with Shaghayegh's help she might be able to get through those difficult moments..

At the entrance to the lounge she saw Hormoz's family and showed them to Shaghayegh. Shaghayegh started walking towards them and Alaleh began to tremble. Shaghayegh, who could feel her mother trembling, turned her head and gave her an angry look. Alaleh tried to compose herself and behave normally. She whispered: "The self confidence mask" and smiled. She pulled her arm away from Shaghayegh, took a deep breath, walked very confidently towards Hormoz's mother and said: "I am Alaleh, I was in the same class as Hormoz at university and this is my daughter, Shaghayegh." Hormoz's mother looked at her hesitantly for a few seconds and suddenly she recognised her. She held her hand to her and kissed her cheeks and said: "My God, how time has flown and what a lovely lady you have become." Alaleh felt she owed her an explanation but wasn't in the mood, so she just smiled at her again and stood beside them and allowed the rest of the family to ask the old lady her name and who she was. Now she had regained her composure and standing next to Shaghayegh she wasn't afraid of anything. She stood and watched the big screen showing inside the transit area. Once again her heart began to pound.

Shaghayegh held her arm and squeezed it gently. Hormoz's mother asked: "Is she your daughter?" Alaleh said: "Yes" and looked at the screen again. Shaghayegh smiled at the old lady and nodded her head. Alaleh's eyes were transfixed by the images on the screen. Shaghayegh was following the direction of her eyes and at the same time heard Hormoz's mother say: "Oh God bless you my darling." Shaghayegh was about to laugh. On the big screen a man of middling height with thinning hair was picking up a suitcase from the conveyor belt. Shaghayegh turned her head and looked at Alaleh. Alaleh's eyes had narrowed and she was about to cry at any moment. Shaghayegh poked her gently on the side of her waist and said: "Be careful not to lose your lenses." Now he could no longer be seen on the big screen. Alaleh was looking at the line of passengers who were coming out when she heard the voice of one of the women in the welcoming party who shouted: "There he is; he's out." Shaghayegh held Alaleh's arm and said: "Don't fall!" but Alaleh didn't hear her. Hormoz was making his way along the passage with iron barriers on each side. He was wearing a pair of denim trousers, a Harris Tweed jacket and a long scarf round his neck. He went straight to his parents and embraced and kissed them. Alaleh looked at his face. Hormoz had put on weight; there were a few wrinkles under his eyes and his hair was greying. Hormoz was kissing some of his relatives and shaking hands with the others; he was patting the young ones on their backs and ruffling the children's hair and moving on. At last he reached Alaleh and Shaghayegh; he looked at them for a few seconds; his expression became one of bewilderment and then after a couple of moments and with a voice trapped in his throat from excitement he said: "I can't believe it!" Very firmly Alaleh said: "Why can't you believe it? It's me in every sense." And then the two of them laughed loudly. Shaghayegh breathed more easily now. Her father was much more handsome than Hormoz. After a little while Alaleh introduced Shaghayegh to him. Hormoz looked at her carefully and said: "Her eyes are like yours," and they all left the waiting lounge together. Hormoz's mother invited them to her house but Alaleh decline the invitation saying that it was too late, even though she didn't really want to get away from them. When they got into the car Alaleh said: "Well?"

Shaghayegh wanted to say "He wasn't at all handsome," but she couldn't bring herself to say it so she smiled and said: "It wasn't very difficult was it?"

Alaleh said: "it was a lot easier than I had imagined; had I seen him in the street, I wouldn't have recognised him. He somehow seemed to me a lot taller in those days."

Shaghayegh wanted to say: "You were both the same height," but once again she couldn't say it. Instead she said: "Well, perhaps you thought Alain Delon with Arnold Schwarzenegger's body will walk down the steps of the aeroplane and you would faint, but when you saw he was quite the opposite of what you expected you felt comfortable and at ease." Alaleh laughed and said: "You are so cruel, Shaghayegh, but believe me: when I saw him I felt relieved. Not because I had imagined him in a different way, no, but because it was him: I was very happy because it was the same person I knew and he hadn't changed at all."

It had been two days since Hormoz had arrived and Alaleh was anxious to go and visit him with Farhad. She was waiting for the right moment to ask him. But she knew that in any case she had to phone Hormoz and tell him that she was the coordinator of his programmes. Late in the afternoon on Friday she phoned his house. His mother answered and went through the usual pleasantries. She could hear people talking and laughing in the background; Alaleh bit her lip. Then she heard the voice of Hormoz over the phone; the voice was the same; the same warm voice and distinct tone he always had: "Hello." Alaleh, encouraged by the tone of his voice said: "Hello, it's Alaleh."

- How wonderful, how are you and why haven't you come so I could see you?
- I'll come in the next couple of days; Farhad has been very busy.
- That's fine, I can wait; by the way how is your daughter? She looks just like you did in those days.
- Yes, everybody says she looks like me when I was young.
- When you were young? She talks as if we are ancient; dear girl, we are still very young.
- It may be true in your case but in my case I have aged a lot.
- Oh no, not at all; you are just more womanly and ladylike; and Farhad? He must be a very special man.
- He's fine. We'll come and you will see him for yourself. I won't keep you any longer since it seems you have lots of guests. I just wanted to tell you not to be surprised if you see me at the auditorium tomorrow.
- Wow, that's fantastic! Are you in the orchestra?

Alaleh paused for a little and trying to stop her voice from shaking said:

- No, I don't play any more. I'm the coordinator of your programme here. I thought I might come and see the rehearsal tomorrow so I wanted to let you know.

- That's excellent, so I'll see you tomorrow.
- Maybe.
- Well, stop being difficult now. You must come and tell me all about the musicians, because you know very well I could do with some inside knowledge about their mentality. I expect to see you there.
- Till tomorrow.
- Till tomorrow.

Alaleh put the receiver down and took a long deep breath. She stood up and went to the mirror and saw how her cheeks had turned red. She went into the kitchen. She turned on the tap and drank some water straight from the tap.

At ten o'clock on Saturday morning Alaleh was standing in front of the window in her office staring at a flock of sparrows and the branches of a tree which was now also covered in snow. The time was passing extremely slowly and Alaleh was happy that Mrs. Shirazi had gone to a meeting and wasn't there; but she knew that sooner or later her colleague would want to go with her to the auditorium to see Hormoz.

Time was passing very slowly and Alaleh hadn't yet decided about going to the rehearsal. She would rather watch the rehearsal from one of the balconies high up. She was afraid she might look agitated in front of the others and she was also reluctant to see Mrs. Saghafi.

She sat at her desk and stared at the wall clock. It seemed as if the clock hands were stuck at ten fifteen. She picked up one of the morning papers and tried to do the crossword but she couldn't concentrate. Thoughts of all sorts came one after another pounding her head and then leaving. At last she couldn't bear it no longer and around eleven o'clock she left the office and climbed the steps. She sat in darkness in the corner of one of the balconies. Here even she couldn't see herself.

Way down there Hormoz was explaining something to the musicians. He was wearing a blue shirt with a dark red jumper hanging over his shoulders. Then he asked them to continue with the rehearsal. Alaleh was mesmerised by the movements of his hands through the air, powerful and graceful at the same time, and Alaleh remembered how those delicate hands had seemed beautiful to her. But now the coordination was with music which made their movements fascinating. Then the instruments went quiet and now it was Mrs. Saghafi's turn. Alaleh sat on the edge of her seat and bent forward. She was all ears... No, she wasn't bad. She thought: "It would be wonderful if she played a wrong note; only one note; no, I ought to be ashamed of myself, for the better she plays the more successful Hormoz's concert will be. I am very..." She suddenly heard the voice of Hormoz's saying something to Mrs. Saghafi and noticed how Mrs. Saghafi frowned. A childish joy made her tremble, but this time she wasn't ashamed: "Why should I always fight against myself? Who gives a monkey's ass for Mrs. Saghafi...?" and she felt better.

After the rehearsal was over she went down the stairs and stood at the entrance door to the auditorium, talking to one of the musicians. She knew that at any moment Hormoz would come out so she tried to look very normal. She was still listening to the musician, who was complaining about how cold it was in the auditorium, when Hormoz came out and seeing her came straight towards her. Alaleh had put her hands in her coat pockets fearing that Hormoz might try to shake hands. She promised the musician she would sort out the problem of the temperature in the auditorium and thought: "Now how will he see me with this head scarf and these glasses? Like an old lady, surely," and she turned and walked towards him. Hormoz's look was warm and kind as usual and just like in the old days when they were face to face he said: "How you doing?" Alaleh forgot her anxiety and fear and felt completely calm. She said: "I'm good, how are you and how's it going?" Hormoz waved his hands and said: "Well, the oboe player has got a sore throat and the cellist is not very good and the double bass needs repairing." Then he looked at her curiously and said: "But why aren't you in the orchestra?" Alaleh turned red and said: "Well, I'm not," and since he was still looking at her questioningly she said: "I'll tell you everything later... and by the way I heard your wife plays the violin," and immediately regretted having said this because this was the only subject she didn't have any intention of talking about.

Hormoz laughed and said: "Yes, she plays in one of the symphony orchestras," and didn't say anything else. Suddenly there were thousands of questions in Alaleh's head and she was desperate to ask: How old was she? Was she young? Was she beautiful? Does she play well?" And then she thought he would definitely say: "She is beautiful and she plays very well," and she laughed at her own thoughts. Hormoz said: "I've heard you made a very good marriage and your husband loves you very much; well of course he ought to." And by the way did you know I saw a photo of you when your stomach was this size!" and he held his hand a foot or so away from his own stomach. Alaleh thought: what would other people think if they were now looking at them? and looked at him with some degree of surprise.

- Where did you see my picture?

- One of our friends sent it to me, a long time ago... But now your daughter is quite grown up and in any case I am delighted that he is a nice man."

- You'll meet him very soon; I think we could come and see you on Wednesday late afternoon or early evening.

Hormoz rubbed his hands together and said: "That's wonderful; we can sit and have a proper chat. I think I have hours and hours worth of things I want to talk to you about!"

Now they had reached the door to the entrance hall and Alaleh had to leave him. She looked at him and said: "I have a lot to talk about too," and she was about to say goodbye when she heard the sound of running feet. She turned and was flabbergasted to see Mrs. Shirazi running towards her carrying a file. Alaleh thought: "You nosy creature!" Mrs. Shirazi came up to them and very hastily handed the file to Alaleh and greeted Hormoz. Hormoz, surprised, answered her greeting and Alaleh said: "My colleague, Mrs. Shirazi... And this is Mr. Shadan," and she was desperate to release Hormoz from the barrage of compliments coming in rapidly successive waves from Mrs. Shirazi's mouth. At last she got hold of Mrs. Shirazi's hand and said to Hormoz: "Well, I won't keep you any longer; give my regards to your mother," moved away from him pulling Mrs. Shirazi by the hand.

After a few steps Mrs. Shirazi said: "Why did you do that? I was just about to talk to him..." Alaleh didn't answer and let go of her hand. Mrs. Shirazi poked her in the side and said: "You smarty pants! So it is obvious that there was something going on between you two..." Alaleh looked at her in a rage and said: "Will you please stop talking so much rubbish!" and Mrs. Shirazi, pretending to be hurt, followed her to the office.

On Wednesday afternoon Farhad came home early so they could go together to visit Hormoz. Looking at him, Alaleh realised that he was not at all keen on this ceremonial visit. At the same time Alaleh saw that he had had his hair cut and had shaved very thoroughly, but pretended she hadn't noticed. She was afraid of hurting his feelings. It took Farhad longer to get ready. Alaleh put on her trouser suit, her contact lenses and a little makeup and sat calmly waiting for him to be ready. After Alaleh, Shaghayegh came into the room wearing a brown shirt with matching skirt and asked her mum to tie her hair at the back. Then the two of them sat on the sofa and watched Farhad, who was coming and going, trying on a new shirt each time. He hurriedly polished his shoes, put on his socks and stood in front of the mirror; but dissatisfied with the way he looked he would change into the shirt he had tried the first time and then smooth his trousers. Alaleh found this both funny and annoying. She wanted to get going as soon as possible but Farhad was keeping them waiting. At last Shaghayegh couldn't resist and said: "Dad, you don't usually change your clothes more than once when we visit people, so why is it taking you so long?" Farhad glared at her and Alaleh poked her and said: "Don't say anything; he's just waiting for an excuse for refusing to come." At last when they were in the car Farhad said angrily: "You rush me so much that I forgot to put on any aftershave." At this mother and daughter couldn't control themselves and burst out laughing.

Hormoz's house was quite crowded: apart from them there were ten or twelve members of the family and a few friends already there. Farhad, who was always confident and sociable, was very warm and comfortable in amongst other people. And soon he was in the midst of a group of men and chatting away. On the other side of the room, Hormoz's mother was talking to Alaleh and Shaghayegh about the good old days and the parties and old friends. Hormoz who was talking to some men would, from time to time, turn and look at Alaleh and smile. He too seemed surprised to see her after all these years in such circumstances. Once he came close and whispered: "Together with your husband and daughter you make a beautiful little family." Then he would turn back to his conversation with the others, listening attentively to what had happened in Iran in the years he had been away. He wanted to hear about the Revolution, the war, the bombardments, the political situation and everything there was to know: he himself was surprised at his own curiosity and enthusiasm. When it got near to dinner time, Alaleh indicated to Farhad that he should stop talking so they could leave. It seemed as if some of the guests had been invited to dinner. When Hormoz's mother saw them getting ready to leave she asked them to stay to dinner, but Alaleh was not in the mood and wanted to get home as quickly as possible, to take her lenses out, lie on the bed and think about all of this.

In the car Farhad said: "The maestro seems to be a nice man."

Alaleh said very quietly: "All my friends are nice people." Shaghayegh who saw her father's eagerness to talk while her mother was reluctant to participate decided to take the matter into her own hands and said: "Yes, I thought he would be snobbish and full of himself ut he is very polite and modest. But there was a woman I didn't know who chattered away giving everyone a headache with her foreign trips and fur coats."

Farhad looked at himself in the mirror and smoothed his moustache. Alaleh was gazing ahead, unable to hear anything.

Two days later Alaleh said to Mrs. Shirazi that she was going to see one of the managers about something but instead she went to one of the balconies so she could watch the rehearsal from the beginning.

Hormoz arrived a little late and looked tired. Alaleh thought they might have had guests again the previous night. Very seriously Hormoz asked the musicians to get ready and they began. Alaleh was watching him and the movements of his hands and body which seemed to form a unit with the whole orchestra; she felt like standing up and applauding him until her hands were sore. In her view the orchestra had improved a lot in the past week and sounded more harmonious; now even Mrs. Saghafi was playing well. They finished rehearsing the first piece and were getting ready for the second. The second piece had a beautiful slow melody that Alaleh remembered very well. She had heard it and played it many times. First there was the sound of the violins and when it was the turn of the cello Alaleh closed her eyes. She moved her left hand up and down caressing the imaginary strings and with her right hand she was moving the bow. Everything was perfect; she didn't even play one note wrong. In her own head she could see herself wearing the black concert dress sitting on the platform and playing, and Hormoz was standing opposite her and looking at her. This was what she had dreamt many many times. The cello was reaching the end of its solo when Mrs. Saghafi made a mistake and that brought Alaleh out of her imaginary world. She felt angry and said loudly: "Ah!" and then without any delay left the balcony so that if anybody had heard her they wouldn't be able to see her. She ran to the bathroom and wiped away her tears. She was determined not to get back to the office looking like that and suffer the scrutiny of Mrs. Shirazi.

She didn't go back to her office. She hung around for a bit and then sent one of the junior employees to fetch her bag and left the workplace altogether. She felt a persistent desire to go home. She opened the door and immediately relished the calm and quiet of her home. Farhad's trousers were on the sofa and the newspapers were scattered on the table and the curtains had been drawn making the room dark. Alaleh didn't touch any of them. This untidiness in the house indicating that nobody was at home soothed her spirit. She left her bag on the sofa and went into the bedroom. She stuck the photocopies of the music Mrs. Saghafi had played on the mirror and sat in front of it; she embraced her cello and began to play. At first she was slow and hesitant and her thoughts were disturbed. "How I loved him, how similar we were, but it's all gone; it doesn't seem as if he has thought about me at all in all these years; he is in love with his work. I wish I too was in love with something; something that only belonged to me; to be in love with something as Hormoz is with his work: a reliable love; to be in love with something that answered all your emotions; not to be afraid of being rejected or being loved less or not at all; how I have aged, how he has aged. His hair has turned white but his hands are still the same. I shouldn't think too much about him. Why shouldn't I think about him? What harm does it do to me, him or anybody else? If only I could be young again. What beautiful movements his hands made under the light: I can see his hands; I can follow their movements and like one of the musicians play in his orchestra. I love to play in his orchestra. I want to become part of him and the rest of them. This is a sea, a sea a sea..."

Then there were no thoughts: only Alaleh's hands, the strings and the bow of her cello and the echo of the music throughout the house. Alaleh was no longer Alaleh; it was Alaleh with love, Alaleh with music and Alaleh with all the things she thought had been lost for years and years. When she finished the piece she looked at herself in the mirror; she moved in closer and stared into her own eyes and saw herself staring back. She got up from her seat and felt much stronger; she put away her instrument in its case and picked up her bag and went out. She had to get back to the office as soon as possible.

The next day she went to the concert hall to hear the rehearsal from the beginning; there was no need to go upstairs and into one of the balconies anymore. Now she could sit downstairs a short distance from Hormoz and watch the rehearsal. She was now more confident, knowing that she wouldn't react badly during the rehearsal. From there she could see his hand movements better, hear his instructions and learn about the musicians and their shortcomings. Hormoz was surprised to see her and sounding happy said: "Well, well, what a surprise, I was under the impression you didn't like music anymore, or that perhaps you couldn't bear me." Alaleh smiled and said: "You were mistaken." Hormoz smiled and murmured quietly: "I make lots of mistakes, well, now come and sit down here and tell me when I do something wrong but say it quietly and only to me because if you say it loudly they won't listen to me anymore." Alaleh bent her head and shrugged her shoulders. Hormoz looked at her affectionately but then quickly looked away and went to the platform. Alaleh sank into her seat and allowed her thoughts to take her wherever they wanted.

Her thoughts were mostly concentrated on talking to Hormoz; she wanted to sit next to him and talk about everything and everywhere; she wanted to know how he felt about her, her feelings and her playing; she felt a kind of intimacy with him. She felt the two of them belonged to the same house but had been separated; one had gone away and one had stayed behind and now once again they had come together to talk about their experiences and get closer again. Alaleh thought: "How similar we are," and twisted the chain of her necklace round her finger.

After the rehearsal was over Hormoz came and sat next to her and asked: "How was it?" Alaleh laughed and said: "In my view it was excellent but to be honest I don't like the cellist at all..." Hormoz closed his score and said: "Her playing is very raw and without much feeling; it seems as if she has never heard any nice music." Alaleh said: "Do you remember her?" Surprised at this question Hormoz said: "No!" Alaleh said: "Saghafi, she was a year below us..." Hormoz ran his hand through his hair and said: "Hey, I am dumber than you think." One of the musicians who was close by came and asked Hormoz about his playing. Hormoz answered him very briefly and turned to Alaleh and saw her staring at the platform deep in thought. Hormoz called her name quietly and Alaleh came out of her reverie. Hormoz asked: "What were you thinking about?"

- What I would do if I were in Mrs. Saghafi's place.

Hormoz turned in his seat and stared into her eyes and asked: "Why did you stop playing?"

- Very simple, the faculty was closed, I got married and after that everything changed.
- If I were here I would never have let you do that.
- I don't know; I had responsibilities, the war, the missiles, looking after the baby and work; all together they didn't leave me with any appetite, time or patience.
- If I'd been here I wouldn't have allowed it, I'm sure of that; you were a very good player.
- Alaleh did not answer. One sentence was running through her head: "If you have been here I wouldn't have abandoned my

instrument," but she couldn't bring herself to say it.

- You must pick it up and start again.
- I would never have become anything.
- You always think about everything in an idealistic way; how does this Mrs. Saghafi play now? I'm sure you will play much better than her after two or three months of practice.
- You know that for me it is everything or nothing.
- Alaleh, you are mistaken. Nothing is absolute and perfect; we can only try to get closer and closer to it, but we will never completely achieve what we want.
- But you have achieved it.
- I've got close; I have come close to one part of my life that I was trying to achieve, but in other respects...

Now the last person was leaving the concert hall. Alaleh stood up and said: "We must go, this isn't Paris, you know! You can't just sit here and chat away, especially in the workplace."

Hormoz picked up his music, put his jumper over his shoulders and stood up.

Alaleh rolled the napkins and put them through the new ceramic rings she had bought and placed them next to the plates.

Shaghayegh came out of the kitchen carrying a chrysanthemum pot full of flowers and seeing the napkins she said: "You are behaving like the foreigners."

Alaleh checked her hair and surveyed the table: everything was in order and properly arranged and the perfume of coffee was in the air; she went and stood in front of the mirror and looked approvingly at herself.

Shaghayegh prepared the tea and went to her room to change. The bell echoed through the house and Alaleh said: "Farhad is here too," and pushed the remote control button on the wall to open the door and went into the kitchen. There were a few knocks on the door. Shaghayegh went and opened the door and sounding surprised said: "Hello." Hormoz handed her a bunch of roses he was carrying and said: "Hello, am I too early?"

Trying not to look surprised, Shaghayegh said: "No, no, you are right on time," and called: "Alaleh!"

Alaleh came out of the kitchen holding a tea towel in one hand and a wooden spoon in the other and seeing Hormoz she turned quickly and said: "I thought it was Farhad!" and went back into the kitchen. She came out smoothing the creases of her dress and asked Hormoz to sit down, pointing at the sofa. Shaghayegh looked at her mother who was wearing a broad smile and thought she had never seen her like that. She carried the flowers into the kitchen. Hormoz asked:

- Have I come too early?
- No, Farhad is late; he'll be here in a minute. Would you like some tea or coffee?
- Whichever is ready.
- Shaghayegh, please bring some coffee. Well, how are you?
- I'm fine. But to tell the truth I'm a bit worried; there are only few days to go before the concert and although we have discarded a couple of instruments the rehearsals are not progressing well.
- It'll be fine. We always put all our efforts into the final rehearsals; you'll see that it will improve a lot.
- Alaleh, I've been thinking a lot and have come to a conclusion: I'm returning to Tehran in six months' time and I would very much like you to be in the orchestra.
- Are you joking? Do you think it is that easy? They would never let me. And even if they would I'm not up to it. It's twenty years since I played.
- Yes, yes; it's a short piece; I have even brought the music for you and I'm sure you can manage it very well.
- No, no; that's impossible.
- OK; you don't have to give me an answer right now.

Shaghayegh came in carrying two cups of coffee on a tray and was surprised to see that her mother's face was red and agitated. She thought: "Perhaps she's telling him that she still loves him," and decided not to leave the room again.

Hormoz took his cup and as he was about to take the first sip he said: "So, when is Farhad coming?"

Alaleh picked up the phone and dialled. After a few seconds she put the phone down and said: "He can't be reached."

Hormoz laughed and Shaghayegh offered him some cakes.

Hormoz looked at Shaghayegh and said: "I was telling your mum she should start playing again."

Shaghayegh sat opposite Hormoz and said: "She has, incidentally, started playing recently and she plays extremely well; my dad and I think she is the best cellist in the world."

Looking at Alaleh admiringly Hormoz said: "In my view that is very true."

Alaleh had been caught unawares and without looking at Shaghayegh she picked up the coffee tray and went into the kitchen. Hormoz winked at Shaghayegh and they both laughed. Shaghayegh thought: "He's one of us."

A little later Farhad arrived and was very friendly towards Hormoz. Alaleh thought: "He's always so warm and hospitable," and

Shaghayegh thought: "It's not all that odd that Alaleh had fallen for those two, maybe they have a lot in common." Alaleh brought tea for them and they started talking about the government, the economy, books, music and theatre and ... Alaleh was quiet and just listened, and in her head she was comparing the two of them.

At dinner time Shaghayegh said to Farhad: "Do you know Mr. Shadan says Alaleh should play in the orchestra in his next visit."

Farhad patted Alaleh rather hard on the back with excitement. Alaleh turned red and said: "But I don't know…" and at that moment both Farhad and Hormoz said together: "Yes, you can" and their simultaneous reaction made them laugh even more. Shaghayegh started laughing as well. Alaleh was staring at the three of them in surprise and with wide open eyes; as hard as she tried she couldn't bring herself to smile. She felt as if they had led her into a trap.

On the evening of the concert Alaleh was so anxious and excited that she was about to explode. The tickets had sold well. Everything was in good order and Hormoz seemed to be satisfied with the final rehearsal but Alaleh was as anxious as if it was her concert. She was going to be joined by Shaghayegh half an hour before the start of the programme so they could go to the entrance hall together. Farhad was away on a business and even if he had been in Tehran Alaleh didn't think he would be particularly interested in going to the concert. Although Hormoz and Farhad had become quite friendly and each was full of admiration for the achievements of the other, Alaleh felt that there was a thin glass wall separating them. Alaleh went into the entrance hall accompanied by Shaghayegh. The hall was crowded with university students as well as middle-aged men and women and some familiar faces of well known musicians. Shaghayegh's eyes were searching for familiar faces and from time to time she would point someone out to her mother. But Alaleh was not herself. At last Shaghayegh saw an old lady who was carrying a bouquet of polianthus and drew Alaleh's attention to her: she recognised Hormoz's mother. Alaleh's first inclination was to go to her, but when she saw that she was surrounded by many of their friends and relatives she changed her mind and stayed where she was. At last they opened the doors to the concert hall and Alaleh and Shaghayegh entered and sat in their seats which were right in the middle of the third row. From where they were sitting they could see everything very well. The seats filled gradually and then it was the turn of the balconies. Alaleh felt time was moving so slowly that the concert would never start.

At last Hormoz came to the rostrum wearing a black suit and a white shirt. The silver locks of his hair were shining under the lights and his face was smiling and relaxed. He bowed to the audience then turned and faced the orchestra. The hall fell completely silent. Alaleh held her breath. Following the movements of Hormoz's hands the orchestra began to play. And Alaleh, watching the movements of his hands, entered the amazing world of music. Gradually the hall disappeared from her sight and now she only saw Hormoz, and with every movement of his hand she felt the totality of the notes on her skin. She gradually became part of the music and the music seeped through her consciousness and became an integral part of her.

Alaleh was no longer herself; she wasn't in the concert hall either; Alaleh felt she had multiplied; now she could see several Alalehs: the young Alaleh with her plaited hair; the old Alaleh that she would become; the child Alaleh; Alaleh the mother; Alaleh the lover and the married Alaleh: each in a different outfit and makeup was sitting on the stage playing, and they all were looking at her. One was winking; one was frowning and another one was giving her a smile. Alaleh put her hand under

Shaghayegh's arm and squeezed it. She was afraid that if she let go she would be blown away like a kite.

Now the orchestra began to play a piece which Hormoz had composed. The first bar shook Alaleh to her foundations; the piece was familiar to her, very familiar; she tried to remember the music he had composed for her; no, surely it wasn't that one but it was very similar to that: similar to what? She didn't know but the notes had a taste like the ones she had heard in her dream; they had perfume and could be felt on the skin. Alaleh wrapped her shawl tightly round her shoulders; she was shaking and was afraid that the clattering of her teeth could be heard by other people in the audience. She glanced at Shaghayegh: she was paying no attention to her mother. Alaleh though: "She has become fascinated, fascinated," and clenched her teeth. Then she felt a sudden relief as tears flooded down her cheeks and soothed her; her facial muscles gradually relaxed and she felt calm, and cried all the way to the end of the concert.

At the end of the concert she was completely calm but with very red eyes. As she went to the stage door to see Hormoz and say goodbye she tried not to look into his eyes. But Hormoz saw how she was and gave her one of his bouquets.

The following day when she got up Alaleh felt light; her eyelids were swollen and she had a slight headache but none of these made her uncomfortable. She woke Shaghayegh so she wouldn't miss her lecture and went back to bed and tried to go back to sleep but she wasn't sleepy; she tossed and turned for a bit and looked through the window at the sky and decided she would stay where she was till midday.

She had just dozed off when the phone rang; she thought it was Mrs. Shirazi so she picked up the phone and said: "Hello" in a weak voice; but when she heard Hormoz's voice she sat up and her heart began to pound.

Hormoz said: "Hi, how are you? Why haven't you gone to work? I rang there and you weren't there; are you not well?"

Alaleh mumbled and said: "No, I'm fine; I just had a few things to do so I decided to stay at home and get on with them."

Hormoz laughed and said: "What did you think of the concert?"

Trying not to show her feelings, Alaleh said: "It was very good; especially your own piece."

Hormoz laughed again. Alaleh waited not knowing what to say; at the same time she didn't want her silence to betray how flustered she felt, but she couldn't find anything to say.

Hormoz broke the silence and said: "What are you doing now?"

Alaleh's heart sank and she thought to herself: "What can I say if he asks to meet up now?"

She hesitated a little and then said: "Actually I need to go to the tax office: there is something I have to do for Farhad."

Hormoz said: "Well, now listen carefully to what I have to say. When you get back take your instrument out of its case, tune it and practise the piece I gave you. I'm going back to Paris the day after tomorrow and I will send you the second part of the music next month; I assure you I won't let you get away this time. I'll call you from Paris and you must play the piece for me over the phone. If there are any problems I'll tell you."

Alaleh was shocked and looked at the duvet cover with its flowery design and didn't know what to say. Hormoz shouted: "Can you hear me, Alaleh?"

He sounded just like a conductor. Alaleh said: "Yes, yes..." Hormoz said: "Now you'd better go and get on with your jobs..."

Alaleh said goodbye; she stared at the receiver for a few moments and then put it down. She got up, took her cello out its case and sat in front of the mirror. Like her own hair, the hairs of her bow needed attention and one of the pegs needed repairing. Despite that

Alaleh put the music on the dressing table and played the first bar. Blood was rushing through her veins: it seemed as if it was bursting her bones; it seemed as if her hair was growing very fast and her back was not hurting anymore. She continued playing: the skin on her face felt softer and without her glasses she could see the palest of marks on the wall.

Alaleh played and felt fulfilled; it seemed that happiness had penetrated every pore in her skin. This was exactly what she wanted. She shouted for joy.

On the evening of Hormoz's departure Alaleh, accompanied by Shaghayegh and Farhad, went to the airport. Now she was neither anxious nor worried. She was wearing her green scarf and looked lovelier than ever. Hormoz, who was standing at the entrance to the waiting hall among a few who had come to see him off, saw them before anybody else and went over to them. Hormoz's mother kissed Alaleh and when she saw Shaghayegh she smiled. Very quietly Hormoz said: "My mother is planning to make a match between Shaghayegh and her nephew!" Alaleh laughed. They all started talking about the weather and the possible delay of Hormoz's airplane and the stops on route to Paris. Everybody was talking and Alaleh was the only one who was quiet and listening, and from time to time an affectionate look from Hormoz would rest on her. Then the loudspeakers invited the passengers to go to the transit hall. Hormoz kissed his family one by one and shook hands firmly with Farhad; then he looked at Alaleh and said: "Don't forget my proposal." Shaghayegh looked at her mother but couldn't understand what he meant by proposal. Hormoz was soon separated from them; he waved and went into the transit hall. After he had gone Alaleh did not feel well at all and asked Farhad to take her home quickly.

Farhad said goodbye to everybody and Hormoz's mother once again kissed Alaleh.

When they were seated in the car at last, Alaleh took a deep breath and gazed ahead. She let Shaghayegh and Farhad chat away.

She must take the following day off and take her instrument to be repaired; buy a better bow and change the strings; she must practise two hours a day. She was sure that if she practised two hours a day she would be able to play the piece perfectly in twenty days. Then she would be able to play it for Hormoz on the phone. If she practised two hours a day she wouldn't be able to do all the housework. It didn't matter. She could ask Shaghayegh to cook every other day. How interesting it would be if Shaghayegh married one of Hormoz's relatives... She could practise every day from six till eight. She had to focus on her technique as well as practising. She could soon reach the level she had stopped at and then there would be progress and...

The car stopped in front of a restaurant. Alaleh came out of reverie and asked: "Why here?"

Farhad said: "Because tonight I wish to eat out."

Alaleh shrugged and got out of the car. When they were sitting at the table, Alaleh stood up to go to the bathroom to wash her hands. When she got back she saw a small box on the table in front of her chair. Surprised, Alaleh looked at it and then looked at Farhad and Shaghayegh who were looking at her expectantly. Alaleh picked up the box and before she could say anything the father and daughter simultaneously said: "Happy birthday". Alaleh, who had completely forgotten her birthday, smiled and quickly unwrapped the box. When she opened it she saw a beautiful delicate necklace made of dozens of small stars. Alaleh held the necklace and sobbing said: "I feel as if I have been born again!" She asked Shaghayegh to put the necklace round her neck. Shaghayegh fastened the safety catch and said: "Such a lot of stars!" and sat down.

Alaleh rested her hand on the table and took a deep breath and looked up through the window; high up in the sky there was a star smiling at her.

book identity

Name of book	**Being Forty**
Genre	**Novel**
Aothur	**Nahid Tabatabaei**
Translator	**Amir Marashi**
Editor	**Liz Potter**
Publisher	**Aftab Publikation**
Publishing year	**2017**
layout	**Aftab Publikation**
Cover design	**Nadia Vyshnvka**
ISBN	**978-1981890576**

All rights reserved translator

AFTAB PUBLICATION
نشر آفتاب
2016

Nahid Tabatabaei

Printed in Great Britain
by Amazon